Management Quality and Competitiveness

Christoph H. Loch • Stephen E. Chick
Arnd Huchzermeier

Management Quality and Competitiveness

Lessons from the Industrial Excellence Award

Springer

Prof. Dr. Christoph H. Loch
INSEAD
Boulevard de Constance
77305 Fontainebleau Cedex
France
christoph.loch@insead.edu

Prof. Stephen E. Chick
INSEAD
Boulevard de Constance
77305 Fontainebleau Cedex
France
stephen.chick@insead.edu

Prof. Dr. Arnd Huchzermeier
WHU-Otto Beisheim School of Management
Burgplatz 2
56179 Vallendar
Germany
ah@whu.edu

ISBN 978-3-540-79183-6   e-ISBN 978-3-540-79184-3

Library of Congress Control Number: 2008925414

Cover design: WMX Design GmbH, Heidelberg

Printed on acid-free paper

9 8 7 6 5 4 3 2 1

springer.com

Foreword

"He who stops getting better has stopped being good."

Hans Schneider, General Manager of the Siemens Amberg Electronics Factory, Industrial Excellence Award overall winner 2007

There is a general perception that inflexible labor markets and high labor costs are contributing to a massive displacement of manufacturing jobs and investment from Western Europe to Eastern Europe and Asia. The debate in Western Europe is highly charged, but sometimes ill-informed.

It is true that some low-skilled jobs are moving into low labor cost countries. On the other hand, many more highly skilled jobs are actually being created in the highly developed countries. The total impact on Western economies is much more complicated, and there is some evidence of important benefits.

In this book, we showcase examples of excellent industrial management that has managed to create substantial job growth in manufacturing. This book is based on 14 years' observation of the Industrial Excellence Award (IEA) in Germany and France, the first ten years of which we summarized in our previous book, *Industrial Excellence (Springer 2003)*, and on an additional five years of observation between 2002 and 2007. We have seen that *management's first and noble responsibility to society is to achieve competitiveness*. Competitive organizations create growth and jobs, even in Western Europe. Competitiveness requires clearly articulated strategic positioning, together with excellent execution, and mobilization of all employees to apply their abilities and to pull in one direction. The combination of a clearly understood and shared strategy with mobilization of the organization and execution enables a company to increase productivity substantially. It is total productivity that underlies wealth.

This book offers lessons for managers of industrial firms. It offers a framework of management quality coupled with strategic positioning that together lead to competitiveness. We describe a number of examples of excellent management in Germany and France that can serve as role models. The achievements of the winning organizations have been no less than breathtaking. They have shown us that with intelligence, discipline and drive, the sky is the limit. Success and recognition provide motivatation and good management encourages abilities and energy in the organization and allows it to thrive. Such organizations do not destroy employment, they create it, and contribute to the surrounding communities. Figure 1 shows the employees of the IEA overall winner in 2007, the Siemens Amberg Electronics factory, after they won the award. They are a role model for what is possible.

We conclude by suggesting lessons managers in Western European economies should draw. The current debate is sometimes confused – even senior managers suggest that successful plants that have managed to increase productivity

Fig. 1. Award celebration at the Siemens Amberg Electronics Factory

somehow prosper at the expense of the economy: "Yes, you are successful, but only by stealing business from your competitors and thus, overall, shrinking the labor pool in our country!"

The lesson is that, it is management's responsibility to ensure the competitiveness of the organization. Competitiveness leads to growth and job creation. It is not a zero sum game; it benefits the organization and the economy in which the organization operates. This includes, in addition to management quality and sound strategy, the ability of the organization to collaborate with the stakeholders in the community. We have to move away from the labor cost discussion and the fight over who retains which piece of a limited and shrinking pie. The future lies in innovation and structural change, allowing differentiated strategic positions and generating new sources of value. In some cases, this requires giving up low-skilled work for more customized and productive work that can continue to support economic wealth. The political system must support and re-train the people who are displaced in the process, offering them other opportunities. Businesses must support the political system in this endeavor: businesses cannot thrive in an impoverished surrounding. We outline some of the responsibilities of the partners, government and unions in Chap. 10, although a complete discussion of their roles is beyond the scope of this book. Our emphasis is that businesses must be good citizens in their own long-term interests.

This book, like our first book *Industrial Excellence*, is about management quality. Management must lead the way in finding new sources of value (and thus total productivity) through innovation in products and services as well as supply chain structures, potentially with partners. The three key parties – businesses, politicians, and unions – have to stop blocking innovation by fighting for their own piece of the pie, and support the change. We are all sitting in the same boat.

We argue that business management, in particular, should stop complaining about the other parties and roll up its sleeves to ensure the competitiveness of its organization. That is management's responsibility.

We show excellent examples of how ensuring competitiveness is possible in Germany and France. We thank the managers of these companies for generously giving their time to be interviewed. And we thank all participants in the Industrial Excellence Award for their efforts. We have learned from all of them.

We also thank our colleagues at INSEAD, particularly Ludo Van der Heyden and Luk Van Wassenhove, for their generous collaboration. We are indebted to Andreas Enders, Fabian Sting, and Delphine Delafontaine for their efforts and high quality work in managing the Industrial Excellence Award and giving insightful input into the content and design of the book. We also thank our journalist partners, Dieter Dürand from *Wirtschaftswoche*, and Thibaut de Jaegher from *L'Usine Nouvelle* for their collaboration.

We like to extend our thanks to Sally Simmons and the Cambridge Editorial Partnership, who conscientiously accompanied us during the work on this book, and helped us convert our many notes and ideas into several of the chapters. Her writing and editorial skills are appreciated. Mistakes, of course, remain our own. Finally, we acknowledge the support of the INSEAD Alumni Fund, which helped to facilitate the award competition for the years when our site visits to these and other outstanding firms were taking place.

Fontainebleau and Vallendar   Christoph Loch

January 2008   Stephen Chick

                                                         Arnd Huchzermeier

Contents

Part III: Networked Strategy

Part IV: What Does this Mean? Implications of the Industrial Excellence Examples

PART I

The Challenge

Chapter 1

Management Quality and Strategic Positioning

1.1 The Challenge

In 2002, two managers from organizations that had won the INSEAD/WHU Industrial Excellence Award gave presentations to INSEAD's International Council, an annual discussion forum for senior managers. The topic was "High Performance Organizations," and the two winning companies presented their action programs and reported on their successes, including impressive productivity gains. A participant in the audience, a senior German manager, raised his hand and said: "It is impressive how you are making this succeed, and you are certainly doing very well for yourself, but you are aware that you are stealing jobs? Your clients save costs and become more profitable, you make money, people in India get jobs, but you are using your productivity gains to win against your competition, and so you are destroying jobs in Europe, just shifting those jobs out of Europe and contributing to the flow of jobs to low-cost countries. Companies become profitable, but at the cost of the home population who are losing their livelihoods. How do you feel about doing your country and its economy such a disservice?" His challenge was the start of a fiercely contested debate.

This remark is symptomatic of the direction the public debate in Europe has taken on outsourcing or off-shoring (or "*délocalisation*," as it is referred to in France). This senior manager had accepted the fallacious idea that there is a fixed amount of labor sloshing around in the industry, and that by raising productivity, and by shifting jobs into low-cost countries, that amount is reduced, leading to unemployment.

This thinking is now recognized as erroneous but, worryingly, many people still adhere to it. In our daily lives most of us understand and accept that if something becomes more expensive, we will buy less of it – if the price of beer in bars goes up, people buy and drink less, and if the price goes down, people buy more. If beer is much cheaper in the bar next door some people will prefer to drink there (unless the first bar provides some other added value, such as a more pleasant atmosphere).

The same holds for labor (as well as for capital) in economic activity – if the price goes up, firms will buy less of it, replacing labor with capital (for example, investing in automation). Labor is a purchased production factor, and if workers in other countries can provide labor of the same quality for less cost, there will necessarily be a trend to purchase it there, again, unless some other value is provided (such as proximity to customers and higher responsiveness).

Increasing productivity does not reduce the overall demand for labor. It may do so in the very short term (if, for example, buying a machine releases a worker). However, for the economy as a whole, productivity enhancements reduce the effective cost of labor by increasing the output that can be produced per labor hour. Therefore, higher productivity increases the demand for labor. Productivity does *not* destroy labor. On the contrary, it makes labor more attractive for the economy.

Indeed, economists agree that productivity growth is probably the single most important indicator of an economy's health: it drives real incomes, inflation, interest rates, profits, and share prices. Productivity in the economy as a whole closely tracks growth, wealth, and job creation. Figure 1.1 illustrates this connection through the most widely used wealth measure, Gross Domestic Product (GDP),[1] and labor productivity (the GDP per hour worked).

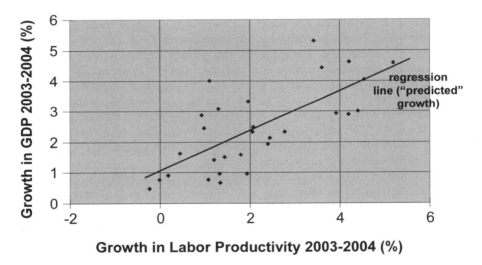

(Source: OECD Data for 34 OECD countries, April 2006; own analysis)

Fig. 1.1. Connection between GDP growth and labor productivity growth

---

[1] GDP (gross domestic product) is one of the most widely used measures of a country's wealth. It is defined as the market value of all final goods and services produced within a country in a given period of time. It can be formally written as: GDP = consumption + investment + government spending + (exports − imports). "Gross" means that depreciation of capital stock is not deducted (without depreciation, with net instead of gross investment, it is the net domestic product). Consumption and investment in this equation are the expenditure on final goods and services. The exports minus imports part of the equation then adjusts this by subtracting the part of this expenditure not produced domestically (imports), and adding back in domestic production not consumed at home (exports).

The chart shows 2003–2004 GDP growth and growth in labor productivity. A clear connection is evident: countries with higher labor productivity growth simply grow more.[2] And this is true despite the fact that at least two other important drivers of growth are missing: capital productivity (the value produced per unit of capital employed), and labor mobilization (the percentage of the population that actively participates in the workforce). In other words, labor productivity is one of the key drivers of economic growth.

In order to connect this discussion to management, we need to broaden it. An economy creates wealth and growth if it is *competitive*. That means that the economy is able either to create *value* (whether this is through higher quality products and services, or different products and services, or delivering them faster, and so on – anything that is valued by paying customers), or to deliver the same value at *low cost*. Competitiveness can be driven by the output side (revenues) or by the input side (cost). A competitive organization can grow because it is able to offer customers value for their money. An industrial sector that contains competitive organizations will grow. An economy with a significant number of competitive sectors will grow. And growth means job creation.

This has an important implication: who is responsible for the competitive ness of organizations? The answer to this is *management*. It is management's responsibility to produce a strategy for an organization that allows it to compete successfully, to be profitable, and to grow. If certain inputs become more expensive, the strategy must be adjusted in order to get more value out of those inputs, to use fewer of them, or to replace the products that use them by other products that use fewer. Organizations that are not successful in instituting a flexible strategy like this are not successful in the market, either.

A successful strategy cannot consist exclusively of managing the cost side. On the value side, it must define unique or attractive services to be offered to customers.

This leads us to one of the major premises of this book: economic growth and job opportunities within a country are heavily driven by growth in productivity (of both labor and capital). Productivity growth is, in turn, closely related to the competitiveness of industrial sectors, a key driver of which is the management of private companies. Economic growth is, to a significant extent, the result of management at myriad enterprises in the economy. Therefore, economic growth is partially the responsibility of managers.

The reader might well object to all the responsibility being placed on the management of individual companies, and point out that governments are responsible for creating conditions under which companies can be successful. This is, of course, true. Many external influences are important for the competitiveness of companies within a country. The government (through regulation, social charges and taxation, the provision of infrastructure and safeguarding property rights), the social system (through the educational system), and the unions (through bargaining of

---

[2] The regression is highly statistically significant and explains 50% of the variance.

labor contracts, including wage costs and labor flexibility) all have a constructive role to play. The interaction between company management and these external influences is discussed in depth at the end of this book.

However, the responsibility of management remains. Of course, management is not solely responsible for economic growth and jobs but it would be equally incorrect to deny its responsibility. Nor is it a valid counterargument to say that a single company and its management team are too small to influence the economy. If this were true, nobody would vote in elections. An individual vote is too small to influence the outcome of an election, but voters have a collective responsibility for the functioning of the democratic system. The same is true for management teams.

How does this square with shareholder value? First of all, we must be prepared to acknowledge that concentrating on shareholder value is too narrow a view. Company management teams are responsible for creating economic value, it is true, but economic value accrues not only to shareholders, but also to the community and, importantly, to employees. Acting according to the wishes of shareholders only is an ideology and an incomplete response to the challenges of the organization, because a profitable company will suffer in a dysfunctional economy, and shareholders are often shortsighted and risk-averse, unable to understand the longer-term implications of company decisions. Companies have an undeniable responsibility to their other stakeholders, even if shareholders are very important.

The challenge that this book attempts to address is how can management teams contribute to growth and employment in the economy, by ensuring the competitiveness of the organization?

Another objection might be that growing the economy (job creation) is an unrealistic dream in an era of outsourcing and off-shoring. Many would argue that in today's globalizing economy, competitiveness requires moving jobs into developing countries, where employees are harder working, lower paid, and at least as competent as in Europe (or the United States, for that matter). In Eastern Europe, India, China (and a growing list of other countries, such as Vietnam) they can find superior manufacturing workers, and even highly qualified engineers, who do a better job than pampered Western Europeans.

The evidence from the excellent organizations that we have studied suggests that this objection is true for some types of jobs, but not across the board. We argue, from clear evidence, that the general view of off-shoring ("Because the wage-dumpers from the East are eating my lunch, I want to use off-shoring to keep doing the same things as before, only much cheaper") is narrow, defensive, and ultimately self-defeating. Companies that try to survive by defensive cost-cutting alone tend to find themselves in a downward spiral. Successful organizations find forward-looking ways of competing and growing by changing and doing new things, not just cost-cutting the old activities. Off-shoring plays a part in many successful organizations, but in defined and circumscribed areas.

1.2 Management Quality

This book is about management quality in industrial companies. We wrote a first book on management quality in 2003, *Industrial Excellence: Management Quality in Manufacturing* (Loch et al. 2003). This book was based on INSEAD's and WHU's *Industrial Excellence Award*, which we have awarded since 1995 in France and Germany. The first book described excellent examples of management quality in execution: what do excellent management teams do in order to make a manufacturing site productive? Productivity is certainly one fundamental lever in achieving competitiveness.

However, we noticed over time that, as knowledge spread from the best automotive and electronics companies to a broader set of companies and industries, that pure execution was no longer sufficient to be better. *Doing things right* began to lose some of its uniqueness, and the cutting edge began to include *doing the right things*. In our visits to excellent manufacturing organizations, we saw more and more that not only the plant manager was present, but also the business unit manager, and that our evaluations increasingly had to incorporate the strategic positioning of the unit, as it gave the execution a unique edge. Therefore, this book is about the second part of management quality, which just began to emerge as we wrote the first book: management quality in *strategy formulation and deployment*. Strategic positioning, and the execution of that positioning, makes the body of this book. However, before we move on the this second part of management quality, we first need to explain and summarize the first part, which has perhaps become less unique but is still the basis for competitiveness. This is what we describe in this section, based on the first book (Loch et al. 2003).

At the heart of the matter lie the organizational capabilities that enable strategy execution. No strategy, no matter how brilliant, leads to value unless the organization has the capabilities and discipline to execute it. As some argue, strategies are cheaper by the dozen, and their logic is generally easy to grasp. The real secret lies in execution, which often requires multiple, mutually supportive capabilities, and this network of capabilities represents the hard-to-copy strength of the organization. Specifically, the organizational capabilities comprise mastery of key business processes and management quality in executing them (Fig. 1.2).

Execution happens at the level of four core business processes: the *strategy deployment process* (the formulation and implementation of strategy), the *supply chain process* (the delivery of products and services from suppliers through the channel), the *product development process* (the creation of new offerings), and the *new process development process* (the creation of new operating capabilities). Performance and improvement across the four business processes, and thus for the entire organization, are driven by management quality. We define management quality through the six dimensions described in Fig. 1.2.

The first dimension, *delegation and integration*, refers to the classic organizational concepts of decentralized action on the one hand and coordinating the decentralized action on the other. Today, unlike in the past, a manufacturing organization is often characterized by complex and capital-intensive technology and the need for faster response to changes in the competitive environment. Therefore it can no longer be run in a traditional command-and-control mode. Management must increasingly delegate decision-making power to the various levels where the detailed knowledge of the manufacturing processes resides (delegation is sometimes called "empowerment"). For example, several winning plants have introduced fully autonomous lines (factories within a factory) with decision power over quality, planning, staffing, and material flows. As one manager in a consumer-hygiene products plant put it: "We are going to the limit of the ability of our workers. I hold many one-on-one meetings with the technicians in charge of projects. They each give a status report and I ask them if they need my help – the follow-up is close. The combination of monitoring and helping not only reduces errors but also motivates the employees and makes them progress."

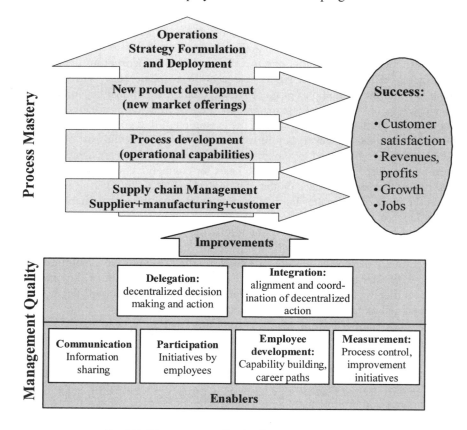

Fig. 1.2. Management quality leading to process mastery

Decentralized action necessitates *integration* in order to ensure the alignment of common goals within the plant and across the business processes. *Horizontal integration* connects the plant with suppliers and customers along the supply chain. Many of the well-managed factories had full access to the customer's production planning system. Several were designated centers of technical expertise for the customer, or lead developers for important components of the customer's products (with customer and competitor engineers on the team). One company had developed such a track record and mutual trust that the customer delegated important project management functions for product facelifts to the plant. "We do our best for the customer, so that everything runs 100%. That's our goal because we are part of the customer," commented the plant manager.

On the supplier side, collaborative problem solving for mutual benefit has become widespread. "We are not here to bleed our suppliers to death. We are here for all of us to do well. At the same time, we constantly re-evaluate them because they can be great today, but that does not mean that they will be great tomorrow. What is beneficial for us is to make the supplier progress with us. Moreover, we have internal programs with regard to quality among other items, and we deploy the same programs for our suppliers. It would not work for us if our suppliers did not advance as fast as us," explained the manager of a winning train control systems plant.

Vertical integration applies to the strategy deployment process, including consistent sub-goals for all organizational sub-units. In the best plants, every worker knew the key performance priorities of the plant and could tell us what his or her contribution to these overarching goals was, in terms of quality, cost, volume, delivery times, or similar operational measures. Often, performance indicators and customer quality feedback were posted at the line, and the workers actually used the indicators to manage their daily work. Moreover, these cascaded goals were not simply announced from the top, but developed annually at every level by the manager with his or her direct reports. The team would start with the deliverables to the next higher level, and every group leader or manager would offer what they were intending to do to reach the goals. If the aggregate result fell short, the team would collectively engage in problem solving until together they had a workable plan to achieve the targets. If it turned out that investment was needed to achieve the goal, this would be at least seriously considered. The process was not one-way, lots of modifications and ideas were fed back from the organization to the top.

Temporal integration of the plant refers to collaboration with new product development. It has become standard in the best manufacturing organizations that production is represented in product development teams from the beginning. Manufacturing lines regularly perform prototype runs, which cost capacity in the short run, but help the plant to give input and to learn in the longer run. A superb example is the semiconductor facility of Thomson, which has become so proficient in testing new equipment and processes that this plant ramps them up and gives them away to other plants once they have been stabilized. Every single production worker is capable of running systematic experiments to find errors and improve yields. Over half their time is spent on testing and process improvements, and yet the plant is highly productive.

Delegation and integration must be supported by four enablers. *Communication* is necessary both to establish an open culture and to coordinate, that is, to equip empowered employees with the necessary understanding in order to make decisions that are consistent with the overall goals of the plant. This goes beyond posting indicators on boards. It includes an open-door policy, regular information about the overall strategy and situation of the plant, employee satisfaction surveys and open discussion of the working atmosphere. This implies a trustful and constructive collaboration with unions and worker councils – "You have the worker council you deserve," observed one plant manager. Information for front line workers must be made concrete and operational rather than conceptual and abstract, but they are nevertheless interested in the plant challenges and priorities and capable of understanding them.

Participation refers to motivating employees to contribute initiatives that go beyond their narrow job descriptions. As a demonstration, one plant manager lamented that "employees who responsibly manage a $60 000 budget in their sports club at home 'turn off their brains' when they enter the locker-room at work." We observed worker-led machine and process redesign where both the initiative and the project management came from machine operators, who were supported only by an engineer. In the best plants, suggestions are not necessarily financially rewarded: workers feel the masters of their own fate and change the face of their work place because they want to, not because they are paid for a suggestion. In several plants, management had put a group of technicians at the workers' disposal, and the workers decided what changes to make to their processes.

Such initiatives must be supported by knowledge and skills. *Employee development* refers to continuous training as well as the existence of career paths for employees to advance to broader tasks and responsibility. The Procter & Gamble plant in Crailsheim, Germany had the strategy of redoubling their output (after having already doubled it) without a head count increase. This happened through automation, with the twist that workers were not de-skilled, but grew with the increasing technical sophistication of the process. When hiring workers, the plant looked for people with the potential for personal growth to higher levels of knowledge, responsibility, and breadth of activity. In the best plants, we saw many examples of shift or shop managers who had started as machine operators and worked their way up, with training and support from the plant, to positions of significant managerial responsibility.

Finally, *measurement* is the systematic tracking of qualitative and quantitative measures of process performance and its drivers, providing feedback and the understanding of where best to target improvements. At Honeywell in Germany, for example, workers have on-line access to all process indicators and plan work, maintenance, and improvement efforts autonomously based on them. Mastery of statistical process control is by now quite widely spread for the purpose of process productivity, but Solvay in Laval, France, pushed the method further: when they perceived a small number of tendonitis cases on the line, they applied their problem-solving skills to finding the root causes of the injuries, and to eliminate the problem (caused by the ergonomic character of some assembly operations). As a result, tendonitis cases completely disappeared. This improved workplace quality above all, and as a non-anticipated side-effect, the effort paid for itself within under a year because of reduced absenteeism in the plant.

This is a short description of management quality, as it is described in more detail in Loch et al. (2003). However, for illustration, let us consider two examples of the power of management quality and employee mobilization. In one of the manufacturing organizations we visited, we walked though the factory, which consisted of highly automated lines with few workers. We came upon a back room, in which four people in blue work suits were huddling around blueprints, coffee mugs steaming next to them. As evaluators, we asked, "Who are you, and what do you do here?" One of the workers answered our question with ease: "We are the electricians for this area. Since the plant is competing with Portuguese sister factories that have lower cost, the plant has as its strategic goal to reduce the cost per unit by X% [actual figure confidential] while slightly improving quality. One of the contributors to this goal is line uptime, which is reduced by electricity failures. Therefore, we have put a number of measures in place in order to reduce line downtime due to electricity problems by two-thirds, and we are now sitting here on call in order to trouble-shoot when one of the new measures does not yet work fully."

What had this "lowly, blue-collar worker" just done? He outlined the operating strategy of the organization, cascaded it down to the line and then his function, and explained how the actions of his group contributed to the strategy. Ask yourself: can your workers do this? Our observations suggest that manufacturing management is currently in the lead; other functional parts of the organization are less capable of achieving such awareness. But the power of this strategic clarity, encompassing all levels of the organization, is clear: operators who understand the context (because it has been translated to their concerns and daily lives) are more motivated and better able to focus their energy. Strategy execution becomes more effective.

In this same organization, improvement projects were common and required three to four workers who would be pulled off ongoing production functions for three weeks at a time to implement significant improvements with the support of an engineer. For example, a highly sophisticated automated production machine, worth over €1 million, had been so greatly altered over 5 years of continuous improvement modifications that the company no longer showed the machine to the vendor who had originally supplied it. Real intellectual property had become embedded in this machine, the outcome of worker-driven improvement projects.

The power of employee mobilization is awesome. The excellent organizations that we observe in the context of our Industrial Excellence Award typically achieve more than 10% cost reductions per year. Of these, slightly more than half come from engineering-driven improvements (such as new machines, new processes, a new product generation with a higher-quality and easier-to-manufacture design). But almost half of the improvements are contributed by the workers who execute the processes and observe all the details of what works and what causes problems. This kind of contribution to the organization's success cannot be enforced but rather must be volunteered by a motivated workforce. Consider another example: an electric circuit breaker producer more than doubled its output with 4% fewer employees between 1996 and 2004, an annual productivity increase of 11.5% sustained over 8 years. This magnitude of productivity improvements occurs systematically in the well-managed organizations that have achieved Industrial Excellence Awards.

1.3 Evidence for the Value of Management Quality

So far, we have argued and presented evidence that employee productivity generates growth at the macroeconomic level, and that organizations with management quality achieve higher productivity. Skeptics might object that we have not shown the benefit of employee productivity and growth at the company level, where the pain of job losses is actually felt. We have shown statistical evidence of management quality driving growth in Chap. 12 of Loch et al. (2003), based on IEA participant data from the 1990s. Let us consider some additional evidence from the IEA participants during the years 2006 and 2007.

Figure 1.3 shows the statistical connection between employee productivity and revenue growth, at the level of the participating organization.[3] The regressions present clear evidence that larger employee productivity improvements led to faster revenue growth at the firm level. Thus, the productivity benefit from management quality offers direct benefits for the firms themselves, where the employees can see them and feel their jobs to be safer because of them; the growth benefit of productivity is not just an anonymous macroeconomic phenomenon.

A similar analysis (we do not show the details here) demonstrates that employee productivity growth is also associated with an increase in profitability measured as return on assets (ROA). Thus, we have evidence that employee productivity enhances revenue and profit growth. The next question is whether the growth is sufficient to "make up" for the productivity: are there still job cuts? Or are there cuts in something else? Figure 1.4 shows that productivity improvements allowed savings in capital employed: companies with high labor productivity improvements tended to have lower increases in capital (fixed and current), which reflects the effects of, for example, more highly loaded facilities, longer running machines, faster inventory turns, or lower accounts receivable. In other words, the productivity improvements go along with better use of capital and assets; they seem to represent genuine enhancements of the value created by people's activities, rather than just cutting people away.

---

[3] Each data point represents one participating organization. The equations represent the estimated regression lines; both regressions are statistically significant. The participants reported changes in productivity and revenues as averages over two years.

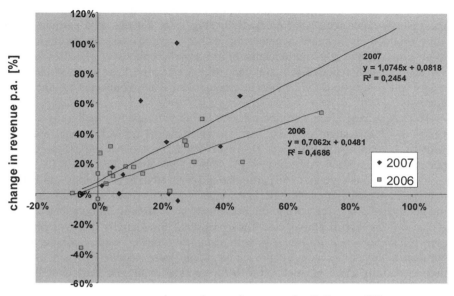

Fig. 1.3. Employee productivity and growth in IEA participants

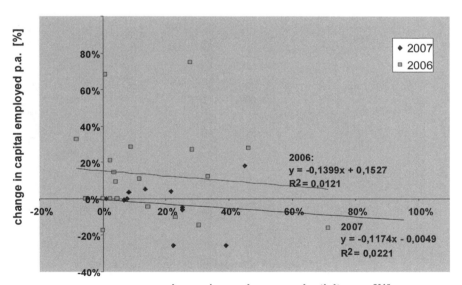

Fig. 1.4. Employee productivity and capital employed in IEA participants

This impression is confirmed when we look at the direct evidence of how employment is associated with labor productivity (Fig. 1.5). For the 2006 participants, a labor productivity increase is associated with a slight decrease in the number of jobs, while for the 2007 participants, higher labor productivity increases mean a slightly higher number of jobs. In sum, over both years, there is no statistically significant connection; the change in employment is not connected to labor productivity.

The total change of the number of jobs for all participants together (over both years) is −2%, a slight decrease that can be managed through normal attrition, without anyone losing their job. However, when we look at our winners, they managed an increase in employment of 1.72% in 2006 and 0.25% in 2007.[4]

In sum, we observe that our participating plants (that is, ambitious and better-than-average plants) grew slightly in revenues with a *constant* or slightly decreasing number of employees, while the best plants grew strongly in revenues with an *increasing* number of employees. They used their productivity gains to generate *over-proportionally more revenues* with a *slightly growing* team of people. These companies invest in their people, make them more productive, and use the increased skills and sophistication to reduce capital employed. And overall, they create employment.

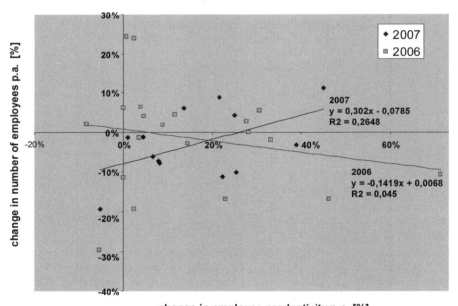

change in employee productivity p.a. [%]

Fig. 1.5. Employee productivity and employment in IEA participants

---

[4] One of the 2007 winners had gone through a restructuring and reduced personnel by 10%; if we disregard this special case, the other 2007 winners increased their personnel by 4.1%.

We have now seen evidence that, at least among the participants in the IEA competition, management quality and high labor productivity *creates* employment rather than destroying it. Well managed plants upgrade their employees to generate more revenue *and* hire people. With higher skills and better processes, they reduce the use of other production factors, capital and materials. Although one might still object that the participants in the IEA are not average organizations (they are ambitious organizations that want to benchmark themselves), we can still conclude that the macroeconomic statement of Fig. 1.1 statistically holds up at the level of individual firms.

Furthermore, if average organizations were to upgrade their management quality, they could also create jobs, without necessarily taking jobs away from the best firms: as the example of one of our winners, Valeo Poland, shows, a gathering of competitive firms creates an industry-driven cluster of competitiveness that builds expertise and infrastructure and helps the entire surrounding economy. In summary, competitiveness leads to job creation.

1.4 Strategy and Competitive Positioning

Although the ability to execute, whatever the strategy, is clearly valuable, as we have shown in the last section, it is just as important to steer this execution power in a smart direction. The definition of success needs to be broader than simply profitability. Although the success of an organization is often equated with profitability (and short-term share prices) on the basis of the shareholder value paradigm, clear evidence from strategic management studies indicates that the success of an organization, as perceived by *all* stakeholders (e.g., employees, management, shareholders, other constituencies), must include not only wealth but also growth, which in turn influences job creation (rather than job losses), and a sense of the positive role that the organization plays in a community.[5]

In this sense, the success of an organization rests on a combination of its ability to achieve attractive strategic positioning and to change this positioning over time as the environment evolves, along with its competence in executing that strategic position. Figure 1.6 demonstrates a *competitiveness diamond*, which summarizes graphically strategic approaches implemented by the excellent organizations that we have encountered in awarding the Industrial Excellence Award.[6]

The interior of the competitiveness diamond summarizes the execution capabilities described in Sect. 2 of this chapter, the first part of management quality that forms the basis of competitiveness. The four external corners of the diamond characterize strategic positions, the second part of management quality.

---

[5] Charan and Tichy 1998; Collins 2001.
[6] Loch et al. 2007.

The four corners of the competitiveness diamond collapse Porter's (1990) generic strategies (cost, differentiation, and focus) into two dimensions (focus becomes a specialized part of differentiation, and the second dimension is cost) and adds two separate dimensions that have become increasingly prominent over the last decade: geographic reach across multiple markets (which provides economies of scale and diversification, as well as exposure to wider ranges of knowledge) and leveraging partners and other parties in a network.

The four vertices of the diamond in Fig. 1.6 represent the cornerstones of strategic approaches. The top, *cost competitiveness*, is a given, in that all award-winning organizations achieved grand-scale productivity gains and cost reductions. Their emphasis differed depending on their business model – some benefited through labor productivity, others reduced material costs (e.g., through intelligent design-to-cost), some reduced supply chain costs through collaboration and information sharing, and still others lowered overheads. Despite these differences, the consensus point is that cost alone reflects only the input side of productivity and therefore represents a viable strategy by itself only in rare cases of extreme organizational discipline and frugality. The award-winning organizations, in addition to cost competitiveness, achieved some unique aspect in the other dimensions, which affected the output side of productivity as well.

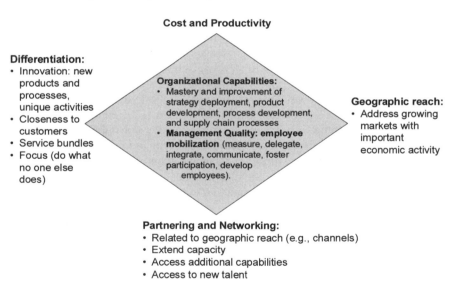

Fig. 1.6. The competitiveness diamond

One path to uniqueness is *differentiation*, or making an offering incomparable to offerings by the competition. We observe four main methods of differentiation:

1. Innovation. The commercial cooking oven company Rational uses as its explicit innovation strategy a goal of making its products obsolete with game-changing innovation after 5–10 years. As a result, it has invented ovens that sense the temperature and moisture needs of the food and choose the cooking settings automatically; the company has become the market leader in ovens for commercial kitchens.

2. Closeness to the customer. This strategy means customizing offerings to individual customer needs by, for example, modifying product configurations or service support or adjusting delivery times and frequency. For example, automotive suppliers regularly place small just-in-time (JIT) plants close to their customers' factories. Although being next door is becoming less critical when information flows reliably, being close enables the supplier to deliver in sequence (each unit customized to the car ID number on the line it will enter). One of our award-winning organizations has placed a dedicated engineer on the customer's premises to troubleshoot in case of problems (including those that have nothing to do with our prizewinner's products); and in addition helps the customer in project management when introducing a new design on the assembly line. Our winning companies manage to put the manufacturing organization in direct contact with customers even through an indirect sales channel. This is accomplished with unprompted customer visits to see how they use the products, by regularly inviting customers into the plant, and with direct trouble shooting for the customer when problems occur. There is daily collaboration with the customer, driven by the customer's needs rather than by considerations of standardization at the supplier.

3. Adding services to the product. Services and manufactured products continue to blur as many companies not only deliver hardware on their customers' doorsteps but also provide services guaranteeing certain functionality. For example, Imaje, a French industrial printer company, has successfully achieved a unique position in the market for industrial printers by adding services to its manufactured products that offer the customer unique value.

4. Focus. In this approach, the organization concentrates all its efforts on certain customers' special needs . For example, one medium-sized company has focused on the niche of assembling printed circuit boards that are obsolete in terms of layout (e.g., they still require hand placement of components, which is uneconomical) or demanded in insufficient volumes to justify investment in a redesign. Large providers attempt to avoid such production, because it is non-standardized, expensive, and difficult (e.g., ensuring high quality in processes that demand hand placement). Focusing on such a niche, which may look unattractive to others at first glance, and investing the discipline to master it can lead to success and job creation, even in Germany.

The right-hand side of the diamond shows *geographic reach*, or pursuing growth from new geographic markets as the home market becomes too small (or stagnant) to support further growth.[7] For example, forecasts in January 2006 estimated growth of 13% in China's and 8% in India's car market, compared with only 4% for the auto market worldwide.[8] Just like car companies, firms in many industries are increasing their capacity in Eastern Europe and Asia (and, to a lesser extent, Latin America) to follow general business opportunities. For example, Valeo built the first Logan factory in Romania not only because of lower costs, but also because a huge new market is being created in Eastern Europe for cheap cars. Additional factories are following in other Eastern European countries. Similarly, Air Liquide has a wire factory in China that operates with older, less sophisticated but highly reliable equipment not to sell cheap wire products in Europe but to be able to gain market share with very cost-conscious Chinese customers.

Finally, the bottom of the competitiveness diamond depicts the strategic lever of *collaboration in networks*. Intense collaboration with highly integrated partners has allowed one commercial computer systems company to unlock productivity improvements at an additional order of magnitude and to provide additional service offerings. Partnering enabled the organization to continue to improve after a limit had been reached on all its internal improvements. In addition, customer service and the configuration of large computing systems with preloaded specialized applications are provided by a network of organizations rather than just one. The computer company orchestrates the network but does not dominate it.[9]

1.5 What Management Can Do

We have asserted that competitiveness can be attained by a combination of well thought-through strategic positioning and effective execution with management quality. How can a management team translate this prescription into an action program?

The answer is summarized in Fig. 1.7. In principle, management has three responsibilities:

1. To formulate and articulate a business strategy, a battle plan that sets out which customers to target with what market offering, what unique value proposition to put in front of the customers, and the core processes (action programs) and capabilities (knowledge) to build.

---

[7] Doz et al. 2001.

[8] *Financial Times* 2007.

[9] Häcki and Lighton 2001.

2. To translate that strategy into lower level (functional or core process) strategies that have the potential to execute the business strategy and are mutually consistent. For example, a manufacturing strategy needs to set priorities among the possible goals of cost, speed, flexibility, and variety, in a way that is consistent with competitive positioning. Translation is necessary because the business strategy is articulated in terms of business goals (such as market share, product offerings), while the process strategies are formulated in terms of lower level operational goals –employees need to be shown how the operational goals support the business goals. This needs to be done not only for control, but even more importantly, to give people the feeling that they understand where they fit in, and thus motivate them.[10]

3. The lower level strategies must be executed by mobilizing the capabilities and energy of the employees, or in other words, by applying management quality.

This sequence of action depicted in Fig. 1.7 is top–down – indeed, this is where you have to start in order to give your program structure. Of course, no one gets this right first time. In addition, no strategy-execution system is static: it needs to change over time as the environment changes. Once you have a first cut, you need to look for feedback and start iterating and improving over time.

Having a conceptual picture of your strategy and execution system is important. But, as a management team, do not over-analyze and die from "analysis paralysis." Strategy and execution are fundamentally iterative. As the CEO of a successful medium-sized company put it, "While the analysis freaks are still staring at the numbers, I just try stuff out [at low cost], and when they finish their first move, I have already iterated once and learned something *real*."

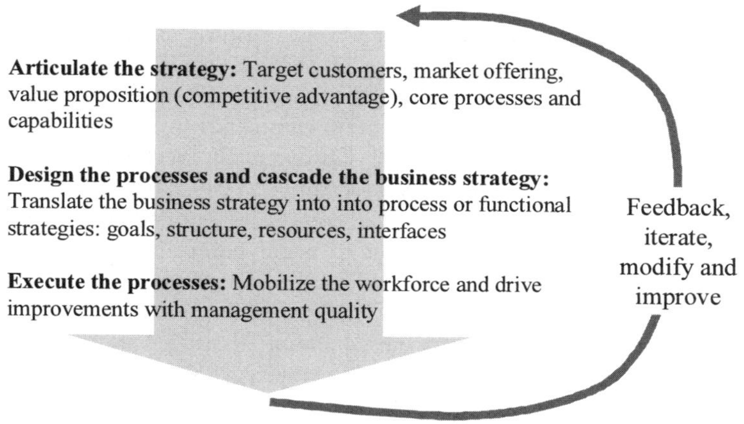

Articulate the strategy: Target customers, market offering, value proposition (competitive advantage), core processes and capabilities

Design the processes and cascade the business strategy: Translate the business strategy into into process or functional strategies: goals, structure, resources, interfaces

Execute the processes: Mobilize the workforce and drive improvements with management quality

Feedback, iterate, modify and improve

Fig. 1.7. The strategy-execution spiral

---

[10] Loch 2008.

We have heard one comment repeatedly over time: "This is nice, but it requires a lot of structure, and structure requires resources, which only large companies have. Your framework applies only to large companies, but it is impossible to use for small and medium-sized companies (SMEs)." This argument is wrong.

It is true that some large companies have put formalized processes in place that help the management teams of their operating units to think of all the things needed to have a reasonable level of management quality. For example there are (in addition to the Toyota production system), the Valeo system, the Faurecia system, the Visteon system, and the Siemens system. The fact that these systems are effective is borne out by all of these companies having won our IEA award (some more than once).

However, executing a formalized corporate system is not the only way of achieving strategy execution and management quality: many SMEs manage the same level of excellence by executing sound principles with cleverness, discipline, pragmatism, and a healthy dose of opportunism. In other words, create your own system in the simplest possible way, but with sound logic and by involving and empowering your people. The many SMEs who have also won our IEA award serve as proof, for example, Steelcase, SEW, Hebel Malsch, BuS and Varta (both described in this book), Cherry, or Wemhöhner. Management quality is a choice, not an application of a corporate process.

1.6 The Organization of this Book

The short summary in Sects. 2–4 describes management levers that companies may pump to be competitive and successful: strategic positioning and internal learning and execution capabilities. We now turn to the organization of this book, which demonstrates the various strategic positions adopted by excellent companies. Figure 1.8 summarizes the chapters in the framework of the competitiveness diamond.

A pure cost competition position is rare in companies in Europe, and none of our winners has adopted such a position. However, all excellent companies are cost competitive, not by being unique but by being "in the game." Thus, we do not have a chapter on productivity; however, all companies featured here innovate and pursue continuous improvement in order to avoid falling behind on cost. The chapters are arranged thematically and reflect the other three points of the competitiveness diamond. Of course, none of the companies pursues only one of the corners with pure focus. They all are strong and differentiated along two or three dimensions (but none in all dimensions). We emphasize the most interesting and noteworthy dimension, while also mentioning other dimensions that contribute to the competitiveness of the company's position.

Part II of this book, Chaps. 2–4, addresses the left-hand corner of the diamond. Chapter 2 describes a breakthrough innovation strategy on the example of the German company Rational, who have set themselves the goal of never being caught

Cost and productivity:
All chapters

Differentiation:
- Innovation: Chapter 2 (Rational)
- Closeness to customers and services: Chapter 3 (Imaje)
- Focus: Chapter 4 (BuS)

Management Quality in Execution: *Industrial Excellence: Management Quality in Manufacturing,* Springer 2003

Geographic Reach:
Chapter 5 (Varta)

Partnering and Collaboration Through:
Networking
- Collaboration with partners: Chapter 6 (HP)
- Supply chain partnering and outsourcing: Chapter 7 (Fujitsu Siemens)
Offshoring
- Knowledge comes back from the low cost location: Chapter 8 (RDME)
- Offshoring and value-oriented service providers: Chapter 9 (Zyme and Dyson)

Lessons for managers and implications for the dialogue with policy makers, the education system and unions: Chapter 10

Fig. 1.8. Organization of this book in the competitiveness diamond framework

in the rat race of mature products, and try to make their own products obsolete every 7 years in order to remain unique in the industry.

Chapter 3 describes the case of Imaje, a French company that has achieved a unique position in the market for industrial printers by increasing its proximity to its customers and adding services to its manufactured products that offer the customer unique value.

Chapter 4 describes BuS, a medium-sized company in Saxony that has focused on assembling printed circuit boards (PCBs) in a great variety of small series, too large to be made in-house by their customers and too small to be outsourced to the Far East. Along with competence, flexibility and reliability, this positioning has allowed this company to thrive in former Eastern Germany. Focusing on such a niche (which at first glance may look unattractive to others) and investing the discipline to master the niche can lead to success and job creation, even in Germany.

Part III of this book gives examples of the right-hand side and the bottom of the competitiveness diamond, summarizing networked strategies in various forms. Chapter 5 discusses an example of global positioning that allows a medium-sized company to address the booming Asian markets. This is the microbattery maker Varta in Schwaben, which continuously innovates in technology. They make cutting edge batteries at home and simpler batteries in East Asia, in order to address the exploding market there. In the past, they moved production back and forth according to where it best fit the market needs (cost versus responsiveness).

Chapter 6 shows how intense collaboration with highly integrated partners has allowed Hewlett Packard's large systems plant in Herrenberg, Germany, to unlock an additional order of magnitude in productivity improvements as well as added service offerings. Partnering allowed the organization to continue to improve after all internal improvements had been driven to the limit. The customer service offering, large computing systems with specialized applications pre-loaded for the customer, is provided by a network of organizations rather than one. The HP organization orchestrated the network, but did not dominate it.

Chapter 7 showcases another type of network strategy: Fujitsu Siemens has been able to not only survive, but be successful and gain market share, in the cutthroat PC business in the high-cost location of Augsburg, Bavaria. This required a combination of excellent execution of productivity improvements (an example of worker motivation and continuous improvements with internal management quality) with cost-oriented product design and outsourcing of non-core activities to service providers.

Part IV of the book turns directly to the debate about off-shoring touched on in the first section of this chapter. The question is whether productivity improvements in companies create or destroy jobs. We first show an example illustrating that, if it happens at all, the one-sided flow of jobs and knowledge to so-called developing countries is only temporary. Chapter 8 shows an example of "reverse offshoring" from a so-called developing country into France: the Brazilian company CVRD, one of the world's largest natural resources producers (iron ore, copper, manganese and other metals), used its global capabilities to purchase a loss-making manganese smelter outside Dunkerque in France and turned it around into a thriving, optimistic, and proud enterprise. This is a wonderful example how expertise can flow in a global company from one location to another, and that the Europeans (and Americans) do not have a monopoly in management expertise: the so-called developing countries are beginning to show Europe that they are leading in at least some areas. In other words, in the long run the game is specialization and trade of expertise, from which all parties gain in the end.

Chapter 9 shows evidence on the effects of off-shoring. We show the example of Zyme Solutions, a value-oriented service provider that creates jobs on both sides of the Pacific, both in the United States and in India, and of Dyson, a British company that used off-shoring as a manufacturing strategy. We then present systematic evidence that off-shoring, if used strategically rather than simply as a cost reduction measure, can help a company on all sides of the competitiveness diamond, and create value and jobs, both for the company and for the home country.

In Chap. 10, we derive lessons for senior managers. In a nutshell, managers will have to embrace their share of responsibility for employment, because no one can be successful in an impoverished society. Companies cannot do this alone; politicians, the education system, and the unions must each play a part. However, companies must face up to their responsibilities publicly and reach out more to collaborate with those parties. If they don't, they will lose the public debate and be punished by politics, or society (witness the radical nationalization initiatives in Bolivia announced in May 2006). When that happens, everyone loses. It is our common challenge to not let things go that far.

PART II

Management Quality, Innovation, and Services

Chapter 2

Rational: Innovation and Game-Changing Products

Rational provides an example of a company that has made innovation and continuous improvement the cornerstones of its strategy. Rational, a maker of professional cooking equipment, relentlessly pursues improvement in all its processes. Moreover, it strives to make its own products obsolete by offering a radical innovation with a step-change improvement every 7 years or so. The result is world market leadership for this medium-sized company.

2.1 The Rational Way

2.1.1 Anyone Can Cook

Cooking on a large scale is nothing like the process that takes place in the domestic kitchen. A professional kitchen is a job-shop or batch-processing factory in which large quantities of food must be hand-crafted to a consistent standard and delivered quickly and efficiently. It runs on discipline and teamwork, with its staff exposed to high levels of stress one minute and the boredom of mindless routine chores the next. That, at least, is the traditional view. These days, a growing number of professional kitchens employ modern appliances that can save a great deal of the painstaking manual work. They can even banish the stress and anxiety created when a sauce curdles or a hundred soufflés deflate.

Rational, a medium-sized company based in Landsberg am Lech, Germany, is one of the world's leading manufacturers of this new generation of professional kitchen equipment. It is not a name most people would recognize as a maker of ovens; but then Rational does not supply the household market. In the catering trade, however, the Rational brand name is recognized instantly – or rather its products are. The company is famous among professional chefs for its Self-Cooking Center (SCC) and its Vario ovens (also known as VarioCooking Centers or VCC).

Rational is a remarkable company for a number of reasons. One of the more surprising is that fact that it has just two product lines – in defiance of what many business-people would consider common sense. In many industries, this would indeed be a risky strategy, but Rational's chosen environment is not a fickle market subject to changing whims and fashions. People need to eat, and kitchens need to cook: there will always be a demand for ovens. Rational CEO Dr. Gunter Blaschke explains, "We're not interested in producing umpteen products: just one or two perfect ones. We want to be the Michael Schumacher of catering equipment and excel in our own area of expertise."

The products that Rational has developed are certainly ahead of the competition in terms of technology, quality, and performance and this is reflected in the company's market dominance. Although a relatively small enterprise – group turnover in 2006 was €284 million – the company claims the lion's share of the world market for professional ovens at around 52%. Blaschke declares that the secret of Rational's success is simply an "obsession" with the end-user. Central to the company philosophy is the need to instill customer benefit-awareness into every employee. This starts with R&D, which is driven by customer feedback. "Our products give customers solutions that help them to increase their profits and to improve their workspace and simplify the cooking processes" says Blaschke.

Founded in 1973, the company revolutionized the industry when, in 2004, it launched the SelfCooking Center as the last word in labor-saving, super-efficient and high-quality ensuring kitchen appliances. A highly engineered product incorporating advanced electronic control systems and built-in international cooking intelligence, the SCC can be used for an array of different cooking and baking methods. According to Rational, this one unit effectively replaces 50% of a kitchen's traditional appliances while occupying less than half the space (Fig. 2.1).

The SCC brochure invites users to "rediscover the pleasure of cooking … forget stress and routine chores" – a temptation that is surely hard to resist. And it's true; with the SCC the cooking process has been reduced to simply keying-in the type of food to be cooked and the desired cooking result, for example, browning level from light to dark and cooking level from rare to well done. The equipment does the rest: using internally coded knowledge of 40 national cooking and eating habits, it automatically indentifies the type of food placed inside it, registers size

Fig. 2.1. Demonstration of the SelfCooking Center

and loading quantity, and automatically calculates the ideal cooking process to meet the result specified. Training, according to Rational's brochure, is "absolutely unnecessary … even a non-professional can use the SelfCooking Center with no problem [and achieve] perfect results, consistent every time."

Hard on the heels of the SCC came the VarioCooking Center, an even more versatile variation of a similar self-cooking concept. This machine – a tilt pan, boiling pan, and deep-fat fryer all in one – is made by Rational's French subsidiary, Frima (Fig. 2.2). Cooking time, temperature, and complex cooking procedures are monitored and when it is time for some human intervention – for example, to turn the lamb chops – the cooker alerts the chef. The whole process is monitored every second to ensure the exact degree of cooking is achieved.

Thus Rational's products effectively de-skill many traditional kitchen functions and are a boon to any mass-catering organization. Fast-food outlets therefore have embraced the SCC and VCC concepts with enthusiasm. Perhaps surprisingly, so has the world of *haute cuisine* – the one area where attempts to de-skill and automate the food preparation process might be expect to meet with some resistance. Nevertheless, Rational SCC and VCC cookers are used by establishments as diverse as Fort Knox, Buckingham Palace, and the Kremlin, as well as many top restaurants, including those of revered French chef Paul Bocuse. Every day more than 85 million meals are prepared in Rational machines in countries the world over: about 80% of the company's products are exported – the majority to Europe, the United States, Japan and China – a trend that is on the rise.

Fig. 2.2. Demonstration of the VarioCooking Center

2.1.2 Success to Date

Rational's desire to produce just one "perfect" product, one within Rational and one within FRIMA, rather than a whole range of diversified products, means that all its R&D effort is concentrated into a very narrow field. The result is a highly advanced machine incorporating technology that is continually reviewed and updated. Without another product line with which to spread the risk, Rational has to ensure that its products are at least one step ahead of the competition in all respects. By focusing exclusively on one product and one customer category, Rational believes that it has achieved a 5- to 7-year edge on the competition. As long as it maintains its lead, Rational can expect to reap the rewards from a loyal and satisfied customer base, increasing sales, improving profitability and, it hopes, widening the gap between itself and its nearest rival.

Rational participated in the IEA competition twice: the company won a second prize in 2002 for its lean "one-piece flow" in production and its innovativeness. In 2006, Rational was declared the overall winner due to its lean management and continuous improvement philosophy applied everywhere, in all parts of the company including its internal administrative departments, and its repeated breakthrough innovation capability.

Over the past 6 years, the company has grown by more than 50%; between 2001 and 2006 (the most recent available figures) turnover increased from €167 million to €284 million. Annual growth over the past decade has been consistently in the region of 10–15% and the company notes in its 2006 Annual Report that there is disproportionate growth in new markets: "The usual ranking still applies for countries with the strongest economies in the world: first USA, second Japan and third Germany. However, China has now overtaken France and the UK." Rational has identified the key markets for future growth as China, the USA, Japan, India and Russia. Nevertheless, even in its home market of Germany there is no sign of a slowdown. In 2006 the company sold over 5,800 appliances and, with growth there still in double digits, for Rational Germany remains the market with by far the strongest sales. In the first 9 months of 2007, Rational posted sales of €236 million – 19% higher than the previous year's figure of €199 million. Sales in the third quarter rose by 19% to €82 million.

2.2 The Strategy

2.2.1 Knowing the Core Competence

All successful manufacturers can define their markets fairly clearly, but most have more than one string to their bow. Not Rational, however. Rational prides itself on being entirely dedicated to one central function: the basic human desire to eat away from home. This defining role is set out clearly in the company's 2006 Annual Report:

> Our core expertise is the transfer of thermal energy to all kinds of food. So we do not see ourselves first and foremost as a machine manufacturer but as innovative problem-solvers for our customers

and:

> We are specialists because we know that we can serve our well-defined target group most effectively and clearly by concentrating all our efforts on an important central need of this target group and solving their problems – better than others can – in an optimum manner. ... From our knowledge as specialists, we set out to create *more* value to the customer, which creates, in turn, more customer acceptance and loyalty – it's a positive spiral.

This target group comprises professional chefs; and because the company believes it is important for its staff genuinely to empathize with its customers, all members of Rational's sales force are chefs too. Trained chefs are employed not only to sell Rational's cookers but also to help in their design and development: physicists carry out basic research, design engineers work on product design, but it is a team of chefs, food scientists and nutritionists, researching practical applications, that keeps the whole process tuned into the "customer's operational world." By maintaining an intimate relationship with its target group, Rational aspires to become part of their "world" in the hope that its devotion will be rewarded with their loyalty. This intimacy with the customer base enables Rational to quantify its potential market very accurately and plan its growth strategy very clearly. The company estimates that the potential market comprises 2.5 million customers; of these, only 500,000 are currently using combi-steamers. Rational therefore has a clear idea of its growth potential and a clear strategy for fulfilling it.

2.2.2 Reaching the Customer

For most of the company's history, Rational's approach to marketing has followed the customary strategy of canvassing and developing new business. In 2006 Rational's marketing took an additional direction, focusing on increasing the loyalty of its existing customers. To an outsider, the desire to increase the loyalty of an already loyal customer base looks like a waste of effort. But for Rational, which has only one product line, keeping ahead of the competition is essential and that is best done by ensuring that your customer base always prefers your product, and by continuously increasing the recommendation rate of highly satisfied customers to their colleagues in other kitchens. Rational is therefore constantly endeavoring to intensify its relationship with its customer base.

In 2006, Rational commissioned market researcher TNS Infratest to carry out an independent customer satisfaction survey. The result was a "resounding vote of confidence among SelfCooking Center customers" with Rational ranked in the top

10% of the best German companies across all sectors. The SelfCooking Center itself earned the top customer satisfaction score of all: 96 index points; the satisfaction level of customers who also own and use a rival appliance was only 23 index points. The conclusion drawn by the survey was that customers can derive up to four times as much benefit from the SelfCooking Center than with a competitor's combi-steamer, at the same purchasing price level.

The Infratest survey identified 84% of SelfCooking Center owners as "apostles" – loyal, satisfied, and willing to recommend the product to others. This score was nearly twice as high as the average figure obtained by Infratest in an industry-wide survey. These customers are Rational's best salespeople; they must be looked after, reasoned the company. So in 2006 Rational set up its Club Rational, an on-line club for the company's 150,000 apostles around the world. Club Rational is an Internet-based platform on which customers can access advice and exchange ideas as part of an elite community of SelfCooking Centre users. Recipes, a technical help-desk, and other instantly accessible features are backed with more tangible benefits – such as a free SelfCooking Center seminar to help users get the best from their equipment.

With an estimated 53% share of the world market, one of Rational's biggest challenges is to maintain its lead. Ironically, because of the company's very high market penetration its customers generally feel they have little choice but to buy Rational goods – a perception that can generate negative feelings towards the brand. This is a well-documented phenomenon, best illustrated by the widespread criticism leveled at software giant Microsoft, which some see as abusing a near-monopoly position in the world of computing. Rational has never been the subject of accusations of anti-competitive business practices (still less legal proceedings on that score) but it is sensitive to the public perception of its dominant market position. It has addressed this very cleverly by developing a multi-brand strategy for its products. Rational therefore uses dozens of different names to penetrate overseas markets; for example, in France Rational products are sold under the Frima label, in Europe it is Metos, and in Japan it is Fujimak. Besides creating a more varied image for the company, this strategy effectively generates more "noise" in the market and helps the company open up new market segments.

2.2.3 Building the Product

Rational's Landsberg factory is divided into two plants, one in which components are manufactured and another in which ovens are assembled and finished. During the assembly process, a single worker – in the company's terminology a "collaborator" – is responsible for each individual oven, from the incoming order through to the finished product that leaves the factory, 3 days later, tagged with the collaborator's name. It is a classic lean manufacturing process, physically separated into four factory aisles, one for each major product variant, with a high level of flexibility to allow adaptation to customer requirements. "Each assembly zone is responsible for its stock and capacity planning, depending on the orders it receives," says Chief Technology Officer (CTO) Peter Wiedemann.

Name-tagging individual products not only benefits traceability and quality control but also increases a worker's tendency to identify with the product and take pride in its production. The production line set-up is also a classic example of postponement strategy, designed to respond to individual customer requirements. As assembly progresses, the product specification options increase from an initial 24 variants to nearly 1,000 by the end of the process. But despite this high degree of flexibility and variation, the collaborator system reduces the risk of product defects creeping into the assembly process to the extent that, by 2005, Rational recorded a defect level of just 30 ppm (parts per million).

Key components for the product range are sourced from 148 European suppliers on a maximum lead time of 7 days. The supply chain is not only essentially local but also long-term and Rational works closely with its supply partner in order to optimize product specification and supply set-up. Suppliers are evaluated against a range of key performance indicators, benchmarked and scored accordingly. These data are fed into the annual supplier review exercise and shared with the supply chain. Rational works with its suppliers to solve any problems identified through this exercise and issues a quarterly newsletter to keep suppliers informed of general production issues. As a company with little vertical integration, Rational is highly dependent on the quality, reliability, and productivity of its suppliers for its success. So instead of continually pushing for lower purchase prices, which can often lead to costly and risk-laden changes in supplier, Rational works in partnership with its key suppliers to meet shared objectives and to re-engineer products when required.

In keeping with its philosophy of continual improvement, Rational's new product development strategy is reviewed every 6 months in relation to customer feedback – or "application counseling" – gathered from the sales and marketing team. "It is the connection between application counseling and product management that generates ideas for continuous improvement," says Blaschke. The aim is to generate a constant flow of new ideas so that product obsolescence revolves on a 7-year cycle. "We ask the customers regularly how happy they are and check then with the support people and the application counselors. We constantly ask the customer for ideas for modify the product and we constantly modify all processes – it's no good just modifying the plant; all processes have to follow suit," says Blaschke.

Product development and modification produces many beneficial improvements to a new product in the first 2 or 3 years after its launch; after that, further development effort delivers decreasing returns. After 6 of 7 years, a product will have reached its optimum development stage and a "quantum leap" in product innovation is required to re-energise the market, keep customer loyalty keen and follow the desired growth curve. "We must never get into market saturation," says Blaschke.

Rational has an applied science department of 25 people, a product development department of 25, an application counseling group that advises salespeople on complex customization problems, and product managers who perform the marketing function. The heads of all groups meet twice a year for strategy discussions. Quantum leap innovation is driven by challenging goals set by management. In order to come up with the initial idea of the self-cooking center, the management team started with a necessary trend toward simplification. Blaschke: "Our old product had more and more dials and parameters, they overtaxed the customer and were too hard to use. We needed to find a way to recognize and program trends and patterns into the machines." The vision became "a machine with only one button."

At first, the chefs were resistant: it would be impossible, no one knew the patterns in *haute cuisine* cooking. But management insisted. Then, the applied science group ran trials for an entire year, recording cooking modes and outcomes in the lab in hundreds of trials. And they did find patterns. They exploited these patterns by constructing a database with a multi-dimensional space of temperature–humidity–pressure–gradient–radiation (and more) parameters, like a control surface in car engine management. Finally, they hired software specialists who translated this knowledge into control software for an intelligent cooking center. As the machine was now software driven, the usage of the hardware became simpler.

In the end, they did not get down to just one button. Nor did they reach their original 26% hardware cost reduction goal. But the machine became much simpler to operate for the customer, much more flexible and functional, and they reached a 23% cost reduction. The original management challenge had forced them to abandon their old assumptions and develop a machine that was initially thought to be impossible.

To get to this point you need to be relentless. Whenever someone said, "I can't do it," the answer from management was, "Why? What's stopping you? What are alternatives? If this doesn't work, can we think of something else that will work?" Over time, this has created a culture where everyone pitches in, and where people do not give up. They almost always find *some* way around the problem. And people like it.

Currently, the innovation team is thinking about the next breakthrough. We cannot say what it is, but once again it involves a management challenge aiming at an identifiable revolution of the customer's workday that would result in a large value increase.

2.3 Leadership

The system works because it is infused with leadership rather than just management.

We develop our people to achieve things that no other company can do.

Never copy what others do.

– *Günter Blaschke*

Rational is co-managed by Dr. Günter Blaschke, the CEO, Peter Wiedemann, the CTO, and Erich Baumgärtner, the CFO. They have adjacent offices, putting their head round each other's door numerous times every day to coordinate informally. "There are no walls here," says Blaschke.

Peter Wiedemann is "Mr. One-Piece Flow," the force behind Rational's encompassing lean management philosophy, which they started in production and have applied successively in all processes, including administration. Erich Baumgärtner joined Rational in 1998 as CFO, arriving from Digital Equipment with a broad international experience in finance and administration. Günter Blaschke comes from the marketing and sales side. He joined Rational as managing director in 1997 from boiler manufacturer Vaillant, becoming CEO in 1999.

The company Blaschke joined was successful and profitable, but had reached a stage in its development where complacency threatened to undermine future growth. Customers seemed satisfied with the product, and the sales effort was losing focus. "When I got here and saw the German sales force, they all sat in their offices and had a secretary and made one customer call per day and could not explain the product. I insisted on five visits per day," says Blaschke. His new regime was a shock to the system:

> They tried to brazen it out and even mobilized customers against me – so I made them suffer. They bargained with me; then they despaired – the pressure was too high. Then finally they looked around and saw that things had improved. They became motivated and things quickly became better. Now they believe that after change things get better. When we stop changing they get nervous … No compromises. We discuss until we have consensus for a great customer solution. Trust.

The lackluster sales team Blaschke discovered when he joined the company is no more. Rational's internal organization and the ethos of individual responsibility for the product are deeply ingrained in the 150-strong sales force and monitored closely by senior management. Each sales executive is given a monthly classification related to the number of visits made, sales concluded, and future client prospects established. "This allows us to identify quickly any change in a particular area of the market and adjust our strategy accordingly," says Blaschke. Rational believes that "company quality means employee quality" and therefore promotes promising employees from within through a process of succession planning. A highly structured system of annual reviews, target-setting, and performance assessment helps the company identify employees who deserve and want to be promoted.

Blaschke's initial uncompromising stance with his sales team could easily have backfired: a demotivated and resentful workforce is even more dangerous than a lazy one. However, by painting a clear picture of what the future would look like and of the resulting benefits for each sales team member, by getting deeply involved in the change process himself, and finally by changing the management team, the risk became manageable.

What must have seemed a confrontational and negative approach a decade ago quickly yielded results and rewards for Rational staff. The corporate philosophy is one of personal development and the opportunity to grow and acquire new skills is extended to all employees. "We continuously pull our employees upward; if you want to develop, you'll be given the opportunity. We give people any targeted education they need," says Blaschke. He believes that the skills and knowledge of Rational's staff is the company's most valuable asset and so developing the individual is central to the company philosophy.

"Leadership is more than management" is a company tenet. Leadership includes creating space for one's people to encourage innovation, to be a role model, to build trust, to be consistent, and to serve the organization (not to rule). Just as Rational prefers to "pull in" sales by encouragement rather than "pushing" products to its customers, it also pulls in its staff by instilling the desire for personal career development and the acquisition of new skills. And just as individuals in the factory are given personal responsibility for the product throughout its production cycle, so Rational's managers are expected to motivate their staff and lead by example. The maxim for Rational managers is: "Only if you have led by example yourself will employees follow your lead in the long term."

Along with the leadership model, the management team pushes a continuous improvement culture into every part of the company. Everyone has a supplier, a process (for which he or she is responsible), and a client. For example, the controller's suppliers are the CFOs of the country sales organizations; his process is the measurement, data transformation, standardization, and production of needed reports; and his clients are the CEO, the board, analysts, and everyone who needs the data for decision making. Everyone is responsible for increasing the value of their individual process to their clients.

As a result, everyone is looking for good ideas from anywhere (including end customers) and there are no committee decisions. Whatever tradeoffs must be negotiated across departments are quickly settled by the group of department heads concerned, who all know they need to get on, and who all understand the whole and not just their individual parts. When a conflict cannot be resolved by the process owners, there are no standard rules administered by a committee – conflicts are escalated all the way to the CEO, the CTO, or the CFO, who force the owners to resolve them (and tell them in no uncertain terms that they had better learn to act collectively, in the best customer interest, rather than bickering). This allows a very lean execution of operations strategy, cascaded in a personalized way from the executive team through their management team.

Within each process, Rational awards a ranking identifying the best performer – like a sports contest. For example, one controller today supports two countries in producing their annual reports (she knows their languages), and discusses content on business issues with the managers. This would have been unthinkable a few years ago. After a while, as a result of constant change, people redefine the boundaries of what the job means. "We continuously pull our employees upward. If you want to develop yourself, we'll get you the opportunity. We give the employee *any* education he or she needs for the next step."

2.4 Partners and Services

Our discussion of Rational's excellence has focused on innovation and continuous improvement of lean processes. This expresses a relative emphasis of excellence, but does not mean that Rational completely ignores the other vertices of the competitiveness diamond demonstrated in Chap. 1.

First, Rational complements its products with service offerings. A lean service organization delivers a speedy response to repair and maintenance needs and, more generally, delivers after-sales support. During the (targeted 7-year) lifetime of a technology generation, software upgrades are delivered repeatedly, free of charge. Just like a desk-top computer, the SelfCooking Center's electronic brain is capable of being upgraded, and members of Club Rational are entitled to regular upgrades free of charge. They simply order a USB stick, download the software, and their oven is instantly equipped with the latest specifications. The continued upgrades further encourage customer loyalty and increase re-purchase probability.

Second, Rational enhances its growth through partners. While the chefs who organize cooking events are Rational employees, sales are executed through a network of local distributors. After each cooking event, an average of 50% of the participants place an order within the following 6 months. The order goes to a distributor: distributors feel well supported through Rational's activities and generate further sales (without the huge investment in a full-blown in-house sales force), and at the same time Rational develops its own direct contacts with customers through these targeted high-impact cooking events. In addition, Rational administers customer satisfaction surveys on a regular basis, which further strengthen its knowledge of its customers and its relationships with them.

2.5 The Way Ahead

Many corporations, when looking towards their future development, couch their predictions in terms of the external environment. Their outlook is contingent upon prevailing economic conditions, subject to fluctuations in the market, and at the mercy of upheavals in the world markets. For some, this view might simply be a reflection of a prudent approach to business but Rational's distinctive corporate philosophy takes a rather different approach. Rational starts from the assumption that the most influential factor governing the company's future wellbeing is its ability to widen the technological gap between itself and the competition and to remain focused on the needs of its one defined target customer, the professional cook. Having identified the size of the world market, Rational needs "only" to keep its customers happy and to deliver the unique customer benefit message to more new potential customers year on year, in order to follow its projected growth curve.

With sales growth of 15%, and earnings before tax also at 15%, Rational was expecting to achieve gross earnings of €93 million in 2007. "I don't see any limit to this sort of organic growth," says Blaschke. "In an area where there's still so much to do, we can't help but progress. We still have to reach 80% of the potential world market, about 2.5 million kitchens." The long-term outlook is to reach about a €1 billion turnover within the next 10 years by organic growth.

For Rational, growth in sales and earnings should not be confused with growth in corporate size. "We don't want a large company structure, we want to maintain the 'startup' atmosphere, so we keep splitting the organization as we grow," says Blaschke. Typically, Rational is made up of teams of no more than 250 people per unit. "We want to remain a flotilla of small, fast boats – each one responsible and with no way of hiding their weaknesses. Everyone is expected to improve his performance and share his best practice," says Blaschke. Growth does, however, mean making and selling more SCC and VCC products, and with the two Landsberg factories now up to capacity, Rational is currently building a third plant on the site. This new 45,000 m^2 factory is designed to enable growth of up to twice the present production capacity – and for future long-term growth there is an option on a further 31,000 m^2. Representing an investment of around €20 million, the new factory is the largest capital investment in the company's history. It is due to be completed and in production by the middle of 2008 and will provide 100 new jobs.

With its application of process-led thinking to R&D, sales, marketing, manufacture, after-sales, supply chain management, product development, and administration, Rational is able to create a high degree of customer value and generates a high level of demand for its products. This drives the company's long-term expectation of growth in profitable sales, while the path towards this goal is cleared through continuous improvement strategies. The extent to which Rational meets customer needs through technical innovation is remarkable and provides convincing evidence of how successful the philosophy of becoming part of the customer's world can be. The long-term goal – to reach out to another 2.5 million potential customers and achieve €1 billion turnover within 10 years – will require dogged adherence to Blaschke's quest for continuous improvement: "If it's finished, you're finished," he says. "We will still maintain the tension: no leaning back, no taking it easy."

Chapter 3

Imaje: From Products to Services Through Innovation

Chapter 3 adds a twist to an innovation strategy. It describes how the company Imaje changed from a company that sold technology for printing control marks and symbols on packages to a company that offered solutions to its customers. Becoming customer focused in its innovations sounds obvious, but this sort of change takes time and effort. It involved a structured approach to extending products to service lines, in particular by extending product marking to data traceability solutions, and by linking R&D with manufacturing and sales with customer data.

3.1 Transformation Through Customer Oriented Services

3.1.1 The Marking Business

You will have seen the end-product of Imaje's technology the last time you checked the "best before" date on a pot of Danone yogurt or ripped open the printed dispatch note on your latest Internet purchase. Imaje makes the printing equipment used by manufacturers to code and mark their goods and by other industries to track and trace products and services. This technology is highly developed, clever, and indispensable to its users.

Imaje has worked to turn industrial printing, something that is often considered invisible in a supply chain, into an interesting and broader value proposition. This is a challenge, considering that the marking, coding, and labelling of products is often a regulatory requirement (consider EU directives for traceability) and a complication that many users would gladly dispense with were it not mandatory.

Nonetheless, product identification and traceability have become a fundamental prerequisite for most manufacturing industries, and in particular the food and pharmaceutical sectors. Food scares and drugs counterfeiting are, sadly, issues of growing concern in a global economy and regulatory mechanisms are necessary to reduce risk to a minimum.

Nearly every industry has its own requirements – whether a voluntary code of practice or a legal obligation – for product marking. This might range from simply indicating the product name and purpose to instructions for use, list of ingredients, expiry date, batch number, or safety warning.

These requirements are important because information about suppliers and customers means that if, for example, a safety emergency occurs, the item can be traced backwards or forwards through the supply chain. This information can then be used to withdraw or to recall products more quickly from the market and to target these actions to specific products. Look no further than the 2007 mass recall by the world's largest toy manufacturer, Mattel, of several Chinese-made product lines, shown (after their worldwide distribution) to contain dangerously high levels of lead.

Imaje's own core business is the design, manufacture, worldwide distribution and maintenance of equipment for product identification. In 2000, this was confined primarily to small-character industrial inkjet printers and the special inks that they use. They were among the best products available – Imaje had worked hard and invested heavily in order to make its name synonymous with quality and technical superiority.

What Imaje has done very successfully in recent years is to add value beyond simply supplying equipment. In so doing, it has reinvented itself as a solutions provider instead of acting as the embodiment of what many customers might see as an obstacle to their core activity.

3.1.2 A Strategic Reorientation

A manufacturer might be defined by its products but its success relies on a much broader platform of activities. Without the support of essential sales, marketing, and customer services its products will surely fail. Imaje had realized during the mid-1990s that the quality of its products was not being matched by that of its customer service and it took the 1995 acquisition of the French company by US-based Dover Corp to bring about a change of direction.

In October 2000, Imaje chief executive Omar Kerbage called a meeting of all company directors and business area managers to review progress and to identify priorities for future growth. The outcome of this brainstorming session was, in Kerbage's words "a clear defined strategy with a clear view of what we wanted to achieve in the next 4 years." Some simple arithmetic made the need for change abundantly clear: without sustained growth in sales, rising costs and pressure from its rivals would rapidly erode Imaje's profitability.

Kerbage told his fellow directors that remaining passive would effectively halve operating profits in less than 3 years. The company had a choice: "Are you going to focus only on business growth to compensate and exceed your earnings erosion?" Kerbage asked. "If yes, then do not do it without having a clear strategy and plan to support your action."

Imaje decided that it *was* going to focus on business growth. Its aim was to become the undisputed leader in its field by 2004 and its strategy would be to put the customer at the heart of its business, to anticipate market needs and – crucially – to offer a complete service driven by solutions, not just products. "With our expertise, we have the means to become world leader for standard labelling and product identification … because we do what the customer wants," declared Kerbage.

This customer focus has been expressed in three distinct and complementary directions: product innovation, product scope, and service innovation.

Product innovation focused on the continued improvement of existing product offerings. Those offerings include the continuous deviated inkjet technology that put Imaje on the map, and other printing technologies such as laser printing, thermal transfer, and large character ink jet printers, as well as print and apply technology for cartons. Those offerings also include consumables, such as proprietary inks, and ribbons. These products have continually been innovated to suit the specific needs of several groups of clients, including beverages, food, cosmetics and pharmaceuticals, commercial printing, and general industry. Key dimensions for improvement have focused on customer needs, such as ease of use and reliability (which keep the client's production processes operating), and the ability to mark legibly even with oddly shaped packages or a variety of production environments.

The "You make it, we mark it" mindset of Imaje also resulted in an extension of customer focus to a broader product scope. While initial Imaje offers might be used to mark their client's products, follow-up offers would be destined to marking primary packaging, then secondary packaging such as cartons, or even pallets. This drift in scope extends the use of their client's use of Imaje's product from one of marking products for regulatory issues, to applications that influence traceability of products through Imaje's clients' supply chains. In addition to extending internal capability, Imaje achieved this broader scope by acquiring Markpoint in 2001. Markpoint, a Swedish firm bought for €21 million, develops printers for secondary and tertiary packaging applications (boxes and pallets) in addition to Imaje's core business of primary packaging inkjet printers. This was a major advancement of the Imaje strategy of providing integrated solutions as opposed to simply top quality products. Now the company could offer a complete solution – printing machines that could handle everything in the packaging process from start to finish. Figure 3.1 shows some of these products.

The third dimension of Imaje's customer focus process was service innovation. An early initiative was a pay-per-print alternative to purchasing and operating an industrial printer. That has been extended with service contracts to suit customer needs and reduce storage and inventory management costs for consumables such as ink. In 2001, Imaje acquired the French company Adhoc, a software developer with a range of tracking solutions that meshed perfectly with the Imaje printer range. The Adhoc software solution helps to manage supply chain flow information for Imaje's clients, whether it is at the individual product, carton, or pallet

Fig. 3.1. Examples of Imaje products

level of shipping. The integration of traceability software with the enhanced product range enabled a broader set of relationships with clients, going beyond a regulated marking equipment supplier to a firm that also provides solutions for marking and logistics. This increased scope to a broader set of supply chain traceability services in turn required the integration of further new technologies, such as the electronic product code, and the RFID in Fig. 3.2.

In addition, Imaje offered training, a quick response help desk, and financing. The ensemble is marketed as a global marking and coding solutions offering. One Imaje client remarks, "Our business demands good quality, reliable equipment backed up by a responsive support network. The Imaje equipment is adaptable, easy to operate and, above all reliable. If we do experience difficulties we know we can receive immediate assistance via the telephone helpdesk, although with regular preventative maintenance visits from the Imaje service engineers, this is kept to a minimum."

Within a year, the strategic focus was beginning to pay off, and Imaje began to beat its competitors in all markets and improve its profitability. In 2001 – a difficult year for the industry – the firm's flagship Bourg-les-Valence plant near Paris recorded profits of €40 million, which, at 17% of turnover, were 2.5 times higher than its main rivals. In 2002, halfway through its 4-year plan, Imaje's growth strategy received a powerful endorsement when the company was declared French Laureate in INSEAD's Industrial Excellence Awards. The strategy was turning into a path toward success.

Together, Markpoint and Adhoc added value to the Imaje product offering and helped widen what had been a narrow focus on a single product range. The Markpoint acquisition also provided a strategic growth opportunity to increase geographical reach into the Nordic countries.

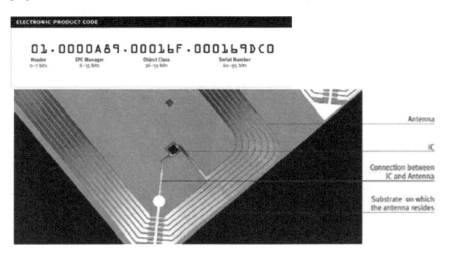

Fig. 3.2. Product innovations include an auto-ID for traceability solutions

These acquisitions allowed Imaje, for the first time, to offer clients a complete system. At Bourg-les-Valence, staff started talking about "Imaje intelligence" and began to develop a genuinely customer-oriented marketing policy. Marketing no longer meant emphasizing the technical benefits of a product range; it was about analyzing the market and anticipating what that market wanted.

"For years the group sometimes did research that was not directly related to the demands of the market," explains Kerbage, "whereas the most important thing is to launch the right project at the right time." This realization initiated a fundamental change of direction for Imaje's marketing department and for its research and development activities too.

R&D was completely restructured and research projects apportioned according to market priorities. Up to 1 year was allocated to projects designed to effect incremental changes in existing equipment; projects to develop replacements for existing products were allotted 1–3 years, and between 3 and 6 years were allowed for the development of entirely new product innovations. Kerbage ensured that, henceforth, all medium- and long-term research projects landed on his desk and were submitted to the company directors for validation. R&D was no longer a spontaneous reaction to outside events – an approach that invariably fails to deliver innovation at the precise moment the market needs it – but was planned to anticipate demand and meet it head-on.

Reorganizing R&D also accelerated the process of innovation, so much so that after 3 years, the number of research staff had increased by 60% and the research budget had risen from €6 million in 1999 to €23 million in 2002. Imaje had discovered a winning formula: marketing and R&D working in tandem. The result was that two new printers and three new types of ink were brought to the market in the space of a year. In 2002, Imaje was poised to launch a top-of-the-range vector laser printer onto the market.

With the reorganization of key functions within the business came the need to upgrade IT and communications both internally and externally. A major software upgrade was undertaken to integrate supply-chain systems and to route some products direct to the client from third-party suppliers. This also enabled some functions to be effectively exported to local sites while retaining central control. Hence ink production was shifted to multiple sites, reducing exposure to the risks of single site dependency and reducing logistics costs.

3.2 Portrait of Imaje

"The world has changed a great deal over 25 years. But Imaje's values remain constant: excellence, innovation, quality and reliability," declares the home page on Imaje's website.

Imaje was founded in 1982 at Bourg-les-Valence, where it still has its headquarters, by French entrepreneur Jean-Claude Millet. From the start, the company's range of ink-jet printers proved highly successful and the company grew quickly to reach the number three ranking in the worldwide printing and marking industry. But like many young, fast-growing business, Imaje lacked the financial robustness to weather any but the mildest storms.

Disaster loomed during the 1991 worldwide recession when a product line, prematurely introduced to the market, had to be recalled. Imaje lacked financial independence and a group of banks, led by Crédit Lyonnais, converted debt into equity, restructured ownership and assumed control. Millet took a back seat and Albert Journo, who had recently sold his own company to Imaje, was asked to assume leadership of the company and return it to profitability.

By the mid-1990s, Imaje was back on track, but ownership was still a moot point. Crédit Lyonnais was under pressure to divest itself of industrial holdings and so it, and the other banks, auctioned the business off through Clinvest, the investment banking arm of Crédit Lyonnais. Armed with a list of potential buyers, the banks and the major private shareholders (including Millet) looked for a new owner. Millet, together with senior managers at Imaje, still controlled about 30% of the business and exercised a powerful influence over the choice of the winning bid and in the end it was the diversified US industrial group Dover that acquired Imaje.

Dover emerged as the ideal buyer from every standpoint. Management was offered both the opportunity to continue to run the company and funds for future growth and expansion. Financing was not an issue. Dover's acquisition strategy was clear and straightforward, and its long track record of successfully concluding transactions was appreciated by the negotiators.

Imaje joined Dover Group as a stand-alone company in 1995. For the next 4 years, Journo remained at the helm, steering the company on a steady course for growth and preparing the ground for the next important phase in its development. In 1999 Journo, who had never intended to take over the running of Imaje, stepped down to pursue other interests and was succeeded by Omar Kerbage, the present CEO.

As outlined above, it was Kerbage's vision of a new customer-focused, market-driven business model that has yielded positive results and enabled substantial growth over the past 7 years. In 2002, Kerbage identified three key anomalies of customer service:

> First, most customer dissatisfaction occurs in the area of service and the business relationship, but curiously dollars and energy directed towards quality are aimed at the product. Second, it costs much more to obtain new customers or regain lost customers than to retain current customers, but most money and energy are directed towards attracting new customers. And thirdly, financial resources on which companies depend come predominantly from the customers' buying decisions, but most corporate energy is dissipated on internal matters that are irrelevant to those very real customers.

He summarized: "We must support the product but we must also support the service. We must get the new customer but we must also make sure the current one is happy enough. And we must spend more time dealing with real customer issues rather than internal issues."

Kerbage posed the question: how does Imaje differentiate itself from its competitors? It had to decide which activities it wanted at the core of its business and it had to choose a strategy to take it there. Did it want to have the best products? The best prices? The best solutions for the market?

Imaje chose the latter and set itself targets – 100% customer satisfaction, earnings growth, long-term viability of the Imaje business, and the continuous improvement of the company's performance. And it resolved to double group turnover by 2004 without sacrificing profitability.

Clearly, such a strategy would require efficiency gains, and Kerbage set about identifying weaknesses in the business. Two main weaknesses were identified.

The first represented challenges in the supply chain. With 30 subsidiaries and 60 distributors located across more than 100 countries, sales and distribution were likely to yield plenty of slack that Imaje could tighten up. Consolidation of the supply chain quickly became a priority.

Imaje began a series of best-practice audits of its branches and subsidiaries and explored ways of reducing stock levels group-wide; each of its 30 subsidiaries was given the target of achieving ISO 9001 certification by 2003. As a means for achieving excellence, Kerbage emphasized "pragmatic behavior and very strong convictions in our means; a concrete deployment of our strategy into operational and individual objectives; and continuous management of our teams, processes, projects, and improvements towards customer's satisfaction and environmental protection." IT was one of the enablers. IT systems were harmonized across the group, and a new ERP (enterprise resource planning) system was developed to manage resource utilization more proactively.

The second weakness was a need for a strengthened market-driven product range backed by customer-oriented service, to complement the prior focus on technical expertise in inkjet printers and inks. Key to making this work was cultural change at Imaje. The strategy had to be clearly defined by all managing directors and business area managers throughout the group and it was up to them to ensure that the culture change happened.

3.3 The Company's Development Since 2002

In 2002, Kerbage's strategy was in place and beginning to bear fruit. "We had made the move from a 'mono-offering,' a single technology and had started to develop 'solutions'," says Kerbage. "We were identifying the most suitable technologies available and packaging them to satisfy our customers. For example, we developed ink-jet technology in-house in 1982 and until almost 2002 that was our main technology. Around 99% of sales were still ink-jet but the market had evolved and we needed to add technologies to our portfolio."

Imaje did this with the acquisition of Markpoint and Adhoc in 2001, but that was just the start. Since 2001 the company has added half a dozen new strings to its bow including laser printing, thermal printing and dot-on-demand. Most of these product developments – approximately 70% – have come from organic growth and Imaje's in-house R&D processes. Only 30% have come from acquisitions. In keeping with the Imaje philosophy of becoming a provider of solutions, each new technology is a deliberate step in anticipation of customer needs. Today, roughly one-third of Imaje's revenues come from products and technologies that the company has added within the past 5 years.

The rapid acceleration of Imaje's product development program is a direct result of Kerbage's shift from a product-oriented model toward one of market-oriented services and solutions. "We asked, 'What do our customers want?' They want good products and for us that includes technologies the customer will be asking for tomorrow. They want integration of the products with their own ERP systems and data flow, including software add-ons. We have moved away from stand-alone products to an integrated offering, backed by customer-focused delivery, maintenance, after-sales services, and training packages. The aim is to have the best-suited offering for all our customers."

Businesses throughout the world like to believe that their customers buy their products and services because they value them. But possibly the most important realization for Kerbage was that his customers do not think this way. Product marking and printing is often a chore for most Imaje customers – their business is producing their product and selling it to their own customer. Marking the product or printing labels is a stage in production imposed by the need to ensure traceability or to convey product-specific data and is often of no commercial benefit to the manufacturer at all but is foisted upon them by industry regulations.

Even the routine packaging of products for distribution entails an onerous identification and marking burden. A simple cosmetic product, like a face cream for example, leaves the production line in a small package – a glass pot, say. This package, in addition to the designer's brand labeling, must include essential product data; Imaje will do that. Individual products are then bulked up, perhaps in packs of 50 or 100. Each pack must also bear the essential data – batch number, date of production, stock code – before being further bulked up on pallets for shipping. These pallets must also carry data such as order number, delivery address, tracking code, date of dispatch, and so on. All these tasks can be performed by Imaje equipment as part of an integrated product marking package. Having to identify, record and print information at each stage of the production and packaging process is potentially a hindrance to the smooth running of the production process.

"Naturally, we're a pain for the customer because identifying their product doesn't seem normal to them – so we have tried to make sure that we do it without being a pain," says Kerbage. Thus, integrating the whole service provision (from on-product labeling to labeling boxes, pallets and then tracking the distribution) into the customer's own systems has become the guiding light of Imaje's solutions-based marketing and product development philosophy for the past 7 years.

"We are not any more a hurdle for the customer … we are not impacting the customer negatively anywhere," declares Kerbage. The focus on complete solutions enables Imaje's clients to improve their logistics, improve the uptime of their processes, improve information for logistics and reduce times for them to react to their clients. Improved labeling may also influence the client's customers' confidence in the client, through improved product traceability, at a time when traceability is increasing in importance (not only in the aftermath of the Chinese recalls, but also following the effects of fallout from the outbreak of BSE – mad cow disease – on food processing).

How does Kerbage know this? The company has prospered, but Kerbage is in pursuit of "continuous improvement" and that requires the ability to identify clearly which elements of the strategy are successful and which might be missing the mark. The answer is measurement. Through the application of key performance indicators, Imaje can quantify the success of its policies in specific areas and make any necessary adjustments. The data come from the customers themselves.

"Customer satisfaction information is integrated into our quality management system. We audit customers through formal interviews both directly via our sales and marketing departments, and objectively via outsourced survey specialists. This is all regularized in our processes and analyzed by senior management," explains Kerbage. These processes are a direct agent of change within the organization, he says.

"We are continually fine-tuning our processes – simplifying them, delegating them – and as a result our processes are becoming faster and sharper." The product life-cycle is shorter and product enhancement more frequent, he says. This was accomplished with improved communication, and the sharing of a limited number of simple performance indicators that focused on the creation of value to customer, on the creation of value to the firm, and on firm growth. Customer surveys and feedback channeled through sales and marketing activities to R&D provide the essential market intelligence to enable Imaje to decide whether or not to develop existing products or launch new ones. "We have full integration of market requirements by the marketing department into the decision-making process," adds Kerbage. New products are brought to market quickly and old products removed to ensure no overlap.

Since 2002, Imaje has maintained a flexible business model, adjusting it by degrees to align it as accurately as possible with the market. This has brought about a gradual shift away from country-focused management towards a business area management structure and a reduction in centralized control. Executive control has been devolved to four regional centers – Europe and the Middle East, Asia-Pacific, Latin America and North America – in order to better address local market requirements.

The practice of local manufacture, customer support and product maintenance, initiated in 2001, has been extended and all resource management is now locally autonomous and accountable on the profit-and-loss account. "But at the same time our philosophy, strategy and company framework are standardized across the group," says Kerbage.

3.4 2007 and Beyond

In less than 7 years Imaje has transformed its business, accelerating product development, reconfiguring its global structure, aligning itself with market trends and pre-empting client expectations. The strategy has paid off. In that time, group turnover has more than doubled, from €180 million to €400 million and, says Kerbage, Imaje is continuing to enjoy double-digit growth.

Imaje customers received a combination of product and service that addresses all their product identification and marking needs while remaining, as Kerbage puts it, "transparent" to their core business. But Imaje's customers are not all treated in exactly the same way. "The customer experience depends on the type and size of customer," says Kerbage. Big global customers, active in many markets worldwide, have a more complex set of requirements than a small national customer. Some require bespoke solutions and the close attention of Imaje's sales, marketing and technical people.

Some 35% of Imaje's total sales are attributable to between 40 and 50 big international clients who are handled outside the "business area" management model. These are managed by senior staff located at Imaje's French headquarters; for many of them, Kerbage himself is the principal point of contact.

Smaller customers fit into the standard Imaje business model, served by local offices and often consuming locally manufactured products. But although devolved to local offices, data relating to these customers' needs are fed back to group headquarters via the sales and marketing network.

This segmentation by type of customer, and by industry application, permits Imaje to set the scope of what it is or is not able to accomplish in an effective manner. "Each sales person is equipped with a marketing tool to enable them to record customer requirements and determine what's available and what's not available. All this information is fed back to headquarters here in France. When a customer has a special need that is not covered we analyze that need against our strategic plan. Has that application been identified in our product life-cycle process? May be not. We evaluate the application on a return-on-investment basis, and if the customer wants it, the customer must pay for it," says Kerbage. "We are highly focused on earnings – we can say 'no' to our customers," he adds.

The integration of sales, marketing and R&D departments is crucial in ensuring that customer needs and market trends are accurately recorded and the right strategy adopted. In this respect, Imaje's marketing department acts as the voice of the customer, speaking directly to product development teams.

As a result, Imaje's manufacturing has changed radically. "We have introduced things that were not happening in 2002 ... integrated *kaizen* [the Japanese philosophy of continuous improvement] and 'lean' manufacturing into our systems," says Kerbage. "With regard to procurement and material handling, we did something special by deploying a global strategy to support services on a proximity base worldwide. This has allowed us to be price competitive and at the same time become more international. This is an ongoing process."

Imaje is now taking this approach to the next phase, outsourcing more manufacture in both China and the US while maintaining an overview via a centralized IT network. While retaining the higher value-added processes in-house, Imaje finds that it can increasingly outsource non-core product manufacture at a local level. "Our logistics activities have completely changed as a result of this," says Kerbage, "helping us to reduce inventories while keeping service levels high and increasing cash flow.

"Today, we are producing four or five times more volume than we were 5 years ago with the same number of people – and that's in spite of having developed more products and increasing the complexity of the offering with multiple technologies." Imaje is continuing its journey to the future after the acquisition of Markem by Imaje's parent company, Dover, in 2006. The combination of Markem and Imaje in one company will help progress its aim to build the new number one in the coding and marking industry.

Chapter 4

BuS: "We Do What No One Else Does"

This chapter showcases a company that has focused on a specialty of complex medium-volume series of electronic components, with high flexibility to respond to specific customer needs. The uniqueness of this approach is a source of success. We describe how this positioning requires continuous skill upgrading to enhance the offering to keep it differentiated, and high investment in process flexibility and quality in order to execute the value proposition. This strategy also depends on the company's location in former East Germany, where infrastructure and skills are as good as in western Germany while labor costs are still just a bit lower.

4.1 Introduction

The German town of Riesa is not the most obvious place to set up a new electronics manufacturing business. The obvious location would be Munich, Germany's "silicon valley" and the largest center of electronics and software industries in Germany, or recently Dresden. Riesa, on the other hand, is best known for its pasta, steel and sports, for example, Sumo wrestling. This town of 36,000 inhabitants located on the River Elbe in Saxony cannot boast a history of high-tech manufacturing—Riesa's manufacturing expertise has been focused on steel, not electronics. Following the end of the Second World War, Riesa became part of the communist German Democratic Republic and new state-run enterprises began to supplement the old traditional industries. Manufacturing diversified in a small way, but Soviet-era Riesa's main claim to fame was as a center of excellence for the GDR athletics team. Sports coaching was centered on the Erdgasarena training institute where, it is rumored, the East German Olympic coaches developed their most sophisticated doping methods. Today the Erdgasarena, and sport of a less pharmaceutically-enhanced nature, remains an important part of the local economy. Oddly enough, the town is now closely associated with the Japanese sport of Sumo wrestling, having hosted the European Sumo Championships in October 2003 and, a year later, the World Sumo Wrestling Championships.

It is tempting to conclude that Riesa's famous pasta must be the performance-enhancing substance responsible for attracting the World's Sumo elite to the town. But it was not the pasta that persuaded Dieter Folkmer and Dr. Werner Maiwald to buy out part of the Treuhand-administered Elektronik Riesa GmbH (the former VEB Robotron Elektronik) in 1991, a year after Germany's post-Communist reunification. The choice of Riesa may have been influenced primarily by the fact that Folkmer was a local man but Elektronik Riesa was an additional draw. The company had shrunk from 1,500 employees to 80 who had been kept on after the collapse of the iron curtain. Folkmer teamed up with Bavarian engineer Werner Maiwald, a former manager with West German electronics giant Siemens, to establish the new company and opened offices in both Riesa and Munich. The company name – BuS – simply stands for "a Bavarian and a Saxon," alluding to the regional "identities" of the two founding partners.

In Riesa, the company headquarters, BuS began the manufacture of LED displays for original equipment manufacturing (OEM) clients. In 1994, Werner Maiwald (originally a dormant shareholder) increased his stake in the company and replaced co-founder Folkmer as managing director. The company expanded into a new production facility and began undertaking R&D work for its customers. By 1997, BuS had decided to close the Munich branch and focus entirely on Riesa, where new production lines were established to accommodate the increasingly wide product mix. Soon BuS had taken over the entire PCB assembly for a major radio manufacturer.

But in 2000 Dieter Folkmer retired, and a new investor, French group Suez Industrie SA, became a shareholder alongside Maiwald. The third party investment was short-lived, however; 4 years later Maiwald bought Suez out to take control of the entire shareholding and recruited Dr. Werner Witte as CEO at BuS. Witte had worked for 20 years at Dräger, a large medical and security company, where he had built an electronics division, spun it out, and managed it as an independent services provider. Then, he had served for 2 years as managing director of the Berlin-based Fachverband Elektronik-Design (Professional Association for Electronic Design). He had just the right experience to lead BuS in making the next step.

4.2 The Business of BuS

4.2.1 The Target Market

BuS is a provider of electronics manufacturing services (EMS); and the reason you have probably never heard of the company if you are not familiar with the EMS industry is because it does not produce the sort of branded electronic products manufactured by the likes of Sony, Siemens or Hewlett Packard. Instead, BuS has carved itself a niche in the business of manufacturing subassemblies, such as printed circuit boards (PCBs), displays and subsystems and modules for OEMs around the world (Fig. 4.1).

Fig. 4.1. Examples of an assembled PCB and of a control module

In electronics, as in any manufacturing industry, the final product is usually an assembly of components sourced from a variety of specialists. Many of these are bought off the shelf as commodities suitable for a variety of applications in a multitude of OEM products and are therefore produced in vast numbers on high-output, high-volume production lines (especially for the consumer and household electronics and automotive industries). Today, this activity is almost exclusively the preserve of Asian manufacturers whose low operating overheads and minimal labor costs allow them to mass-produce quality components at a price that European manufacturers cannot match. This is a long way away from the world of BuS.

Rather than simply churning out vast numbers of standard products, the German company has established itself as a specialist capable of producing small and medium-sized production runs of custom-designed electronic sub-assemblies for a clearly defined customer base. BuS has evolved as a provider of manufacturing solutions for its clients, producing PCBs and other sub-assemblies tailored to the specific requirements of the OEM. BuS's "sweet spot" are complex assemblies in small to medium volumes, too large to be handled by the OEM's prototype spot but too small for the large Asian outsourcing providers to set up a system. This works for modules that allow a sufficient amount of automation to keep the value add (labor content) of a unit low, allowing BuS, with its western European labor costs (although lower than in Munich), to compete with low labor costs of East Asia. What matters is a competitive total unit cost, taking into consideration the sometimes overlooked costs of travel, transport logistics, communication delays and misunderstandings, and reduced flexibility because of the distance.

The reason, of course, is that BuS is based in Germany, not China, and could not possibly compete in the high-volume market. But although it lacks the production economies of the Asian countries, Germany is rich in engineering and design skills and this is the abundant resource that BuS taps into to add value to its product offering. The company has significant buying power (it estimates its purchasing volume at more than €50 million) and boasts that it can provide customers with the most appropriate material at a good price. It also assumes responsibility for all the logistics involved in product development and manufacture. Logistics is increasingly becoming a key decision criterion for selecting suppliers in the electronics industry and many OEMs welcome the opportunity to out-source this element of the business to a third party like BuS. This requires excellent knowledge of the customer's business. BuS focuses on three "pillars": automotive, industrial electronics and special projects.

4.2.2 Successes

Though competing in an industry dominated by fast-growing, high-volume, low-value Asian companies, BuS has grown steadily since its formation 16 years ago. Then, with one director and just four employees, BuS concentrated on producing LED displays, only expanding its product range in 1993 when it acquired Elektronik Riesa and took on its 80 employees. BuS has continually added employment; today, it employs 750 people, making it the largest employer in Riesa. At the time of our interviews in 2007, it was on track to break through the €100 million revenue barrier and is now the largest EMS provider in the former East Germany. Growth is strong, although always carefully controlled; the company has almost doubled its staff numbers in the past 5 years and in November 2005 opened a new 6,000 m² production hall to accommodate increased sales.

Growth has been accompanied by continuous improvement in production efficiency and manufacturing capability. "As we grow, new logistics and production layouts are included in the expansion – that's all part of the game," says Maiwald. And as the business gets bigger, more sophisticated methods have evolved to cope with the added complexity and to optimize efficient production. In 2005 BuS upgraded its cost analysis methodology to help calculate product value faster and more accurately and to obtain an accurate ongoing view of product costs and drive continuous improvements. R&D is located right next to production without a separation: this helps to test and introduce new processes very quickly and frequently. Improvements tend to be engineering driven; although the employees are loyal and well-trained, the extent of their input in improvements is limited.

In 2004, Maiwald secured 100% control of the company as its sole shareholder, Folkmer having retired in 2000. "We no longer have any third-party investor, and that leaves us with more freedom to do what we want to do," claims Maiwald. "We can now be as flexible as a small to medium-sized enterprise needs to be. Our goal is not growth per se but to have a business that we master. We maintain profitability every year – we can invest – and we can grow if we wish." Maiwald adds: "We check our structure and processes to see whether they continue to be effective. Our revenues are growing; will we continue to be as effective at revenues more than €100 million as they were previously?" Productivity, says Maiwald, is difficult to measure because of the ever-changing mix of products. BuS currently manufactures around 2,000 different products and up to one-third of these are new every year. New products take time to develop and bring into production: "The learning curve can destroy productivity," observes Maiwald. Further growth can bring problems as well as benefits, he cautions. Because with every new order the company carefully considers the extent to which it engages in low-mix/high-volume business, it can increase output by adding to the mix. The inevitable complication this entails demands a highly organized and immensely flexible set-up to maintain optimum efficiency.

4.3 Business Strategy

BuS has an unofficial motto that sums up its business philosophy: "Service – exactly tailored to your needs." Service is something that the mass producers of commodity products seldom need to consider – their customers want the products they make and all they need to do is produce the right quality at the right price. But service is part of the product offering at BuS: "You are not looking for a supplier; you want a partner for your electronics," says a BuS brochure promoting the company's service philosophy. "A large customer base and constantly growing number of new customers attest to the correctness of our concept of offering individual technical and logistic problem solutions – from simply PCB assembly to technological consulting to development and production of complete devices. We understand how to incorporate the 'tricky' with the seemingly 'unsolvable'."

From its earliest days, BuS has focused on this service-oriented approach, adding value to its product offering by doing precisely what the large high-volume Asian manufacturers do not want to do. BuS invites its customers to share their problems so that the company can devise a suitable solution. The OEM client can present BuS with a product idea, a detailed performance specification or even an existing PCB assembly that needs revising, modifying or updating. BuS will engineer the solution tailored to the customer's needs. Consequently, many BuS customers effectively outsource a significant amount of engineering (not for product design, but for manufacturing) to the company. For example, a customer who needs a PCB or larger assembly designed to fit into a limited physical space, operate under specific climatic, electromagnetic and mechanical conditions can save considerable time and cost by outsourcing the product development to BuS. The cost of this project will reflect the high degree of engineering design expertise devoted to it; manufacturing costs, especially the labor content, will represent a far smaller proportion of total cost to the customer than would be the case in the high-volume EMS sector. BuS's success, therefore, lies very much in the blend of manufacturing capacity and R&D capability.

"We are a service provider," comments Maiwald. "We don't have our own product range, but we do manufacture. We offer our customers complete solutions, including help in their ability to manufacture and in their ambition to achieve a profitable complete system. However, labor costs do not dominate." Minimizing total manufacturing costs is the key to BuS' ability to compete in the EMS sector: labor costs are an important part, but Maiwald estimates that material costs comprise over 60% of total costs. BuS helps its clients in sourcing and material cost management and to keep other costs down, such as logistics, and equipment. However, BuS needs a certain level of automation in order to prevent labor costs from becoming a problem. Nevertheless, the BuS value-added service is a combination of intellectual and manufacturing know-how: "The pure service can be purchased abroad," explains Witte, "it is the combination of materials, logistics and labor that keeps us viable in Germany. Our product mix is centered at less than 1,000 units per production run – you can't go to China with that. Even our high runners have so little labor cost content that it's not worth going to China because of the quality achievable here and the proximity to our customers outweigh any production benefit. Supporting the process in China is also very expensive except for very large volumes – and we are not in the very large volume market."

Having said that, BuS keeps a foot in the China camp in order to broaden its service capability. An alliance with a Chinese EMS company enables BuS to offer help when a client needs to produce local content in China and is looking for a local production partner; in addition, BuS and its Chinese partner help customers to build their own assembly capacity in China.

Low volume production runs of high-mix products are competitively produced at Riesa – no one considers transferring very low volumes to Asia. But Riesa is competitive in the low-mix/high-volume sector only when the added value component of the manufacturing process (rather than the R&D and service-related aspect) is between 15% and 25%. There are some customers who straddle the two sectors, requiring both low-mix/high-volume products and high-mix/low-volume production; and these customers want both from a single supplier. BuS has addressed this sector through the alliance with its Chinese EMS provider IMI which takes on the low-mix/high-volume manufacturing while leaving the all-important technical, sales support and logistics activities to the BuS people in Riesa.

4.4 Production Challenges

One of the benefits of large-volume mass production is simplicity. You set up your production line and run it without variation, producing an endless flow of standardized commodity products. By being very careful in considering low-mix/high-volume production, BuS has taken the opposite route and consequently its production processes are considerably more complex than its Asian counterparts'.

Production is free of seasonal fluctuations, thanks to the diversified requirements of over 200 customers, "but of course we also struggle with the diversity," comments Witte. "Our sales force is very good at forecasting overall demand, but always struggles at the level of individual customers." This multiplicity of small-volume production runs and the constant introduction of new products into the mix is balanced by a small number of relatively high-volume products – the high runners. These are still small production runs compared with the numbers produced by Asian EMS providers, but they are sufficiently different from the high-mix/low-volume products built by BuS so that they require a separate production regime. "High runners make up about 50% of our revenue," says Witte. At present, there are around 50 of these high runners in production, and they are produced by dedicated lines by machines specific to the individual product. These dedicated production islands operate separately from the highly flexible and ever-changing production process that is employed in the manufacture of nearly 2,000 low-volume products. To help it operate in this atmosphere of continual change, BuS is always investing in new machines, some of which are shared across products, some of which are specific to certain island products. The smaller volume products undergo production improvements and adjustments to factors such as production flow and testing procedure throughout the life cycle of the product. Production of island products, by contrast, is optimized and fixed as early as possible.

Several structures help to limit conflicts between sales and production ("we are very responsive to last-minute change requests by the customer" versus "we need to keep complexity and scheduling chaos at least within bounds"). First, the CEOs decide themselves which customer projects to take – the product mix is a strategic variable. Second, there are two buffers built in production: the quoted customer lead time is 2 weeks, whereas the process can deliver within 1 week for high priority projects. In addition, the production shop has explicitly an overcapacity buffer of 20%. These two buffers allow fast reaction when an important customer change request is made. Finally, the high runners have their dedicated production islands and are isolated from scheduling changes by other products (Fig. 4.2).

Fig. 4.2. Production lines

Flexibility in the manufacturing process has to be matched by a similar flexibility in the workforce. With labor such a make-or-break factor, BuS cannot afford to fritter away its technical advantages by losing control of labor costs. "Every new product brings up to 1,000 new components into our system," says Witte. "We need tools that allow us to handle this complexity explosion without having to hire extra people." These tools include technical and process design, employee training and an emphasis on "design for manufacture." Each product is designed to simplify the assembly process and minimize manual placement of components. But there are also cultural issues that can help. Witte accepts that BuS relies quite heavily on the lower wage levels in former East Germany. But he also claims that, as a major employer, BuS enjoys an exceptionally loyal workforce, praising the "mentality and qualification level of people here in the area, and the support of the community. People here are very willing to work night shifts." BuS also has a very effective bonus scheme in which a profit-related bonus pool is shared according to individual performance review, seniority and rank.

Being so dependent on low-volume production runs, BuS cannot afford lengthy production delays and the entire process from product design to manufacture must be as snag-free as possible. Production planning and engineering therefore work hand-in-hand and both work very closely with sales. By the time a customer receives a signed contract guaranteeing specific volumes, functionalities, schedules and costs, all BuS departments have signed off internally. Sales personnel cannot be allowed any license to promise customers outcomes that have not already been checked and verified. The production planning department checks manufacturing feasibility and issues first authorization; it then checks with the purchasing department to ensure parts are available and issues a second authorization. Only then does BuS invest in the manufacturing process.

Since growth, for BuS, means increasing the product mix and the complexity of its manufacturing set-up, production flexibility is essential. The company's engineering department plays a key role here, helping customers optimize layouts and developing manufacturing lines, testing equipment and production strategies. The extreme variety makes production difficult and the company needs its 20% over-capacity buffer in order to absorb product changes and the commissioning of new manufacturing lines.

Between 2005 and 2007, BuS reorganized production to introduce greater flexibility. The low-volume assemblies and systems are handled as they come on flexible flow lines in small series volumes – typically fewer than 1,000 units. These are sequenced by production planning, which seeks an optimum combination of low waiting time and fast changeover times on the lines. In the largest production building, the lines are built in parallel and at the end of the line sit approximately 30 people whose job it is to carry out the manual element of component placement – that is, the part of the process that is not worth automating (for example, old end-of-life products). BuS is continually looking to ways to reduce this manual labor component and looks to its production teams for suggestions. Flow through the shared manufacturing lines is optimized to avoid production clashes. But although BuS tries to keep production line changeovers to a minimum, occasional production bottlenecks are unavoidable. In these instances, rather than give one product line priority over another and consequently retard production rates, BuS will utilize its spare capacity to accelerate both product lines and ease the bottleneck.

It goes without saying that the broad mix, associated with its complexity and flexibility, does not come at the cost of high standards in customer delivery. These are achieved by extensive testing within the production steps and at the end of assembly (Fig. 4.3).

4.5 Uniqueness as a Source of Success

BuS's strategic position is highly unique in the EMS industry, as an examination of a competitor shows. In 1977, a US company called Solectron emerged from the fast-growing semiconductor industry based in California's Silicon Valley to offer outsourced manufacturing services to electronics OEMs. The company thrived on the fact that competitiveness in this fast-moving industry depended upon the ability to bring new products to market before the competition. By offering this extra outsourced capacity, Solectron could help customers keep ahead. Thus the EMS industry was born.

Solectron is still the world's largest EMS provider, but even this company has succumbed to the strength of the emerging Asian sector. In June 2007, Solectron was bought out by Singapore-based Flextronics for US$3.6 billion. Most EMS

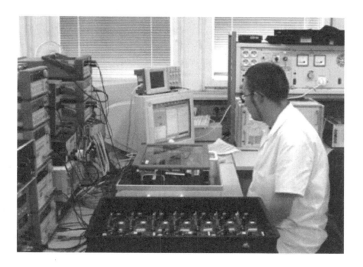

Fig. 4.3. Electronic testing

providers have followed that Solectron model and gone for low-mix/high-volume production. But BuS could hardly be more different and still be in the same industry. The BuS approach to EMS is probably unique. It requires continuously striking the balance between labor costs and other fixed overheads in Germany, versus extensive specialized expertise in customized production along with the closeness to customers that allows flexibility and responsiveness.

There is certainly no threat from companies like Solectron/Flextronics. "We are different. We serve customer in a unique BuS way," says Maiwald. "We target an entirely different customer segment." That is not to say that BuS has not come into contact with Solectron/Flextronics. The larger company did produce products in Hungary, but in a very different way than BuS. "We can adjust at short notice to a very high degree," declares Witte.

This ability to undertake work that nearly every other EMS provider cannot, or will not, do is backed up by a highly trained and highly motivated workforce. BuS engineers and designers have a thorough knowledge of the OEM's requirements and possess product design and development skills that are absent from most other EMS providers. BuS is therefore closer to its customers and enjoys a partner relationship with most of them that brings medium- to long-term security for future prosperity.

PART III

Networked Strategy

Chapter 5

VARTA Microbattery: Producing in the Right Place

In this chapter, we present a medium-sized company with an intelligent strategy of producing in Germany (state-of-the-art products with flexible delivery) and in the Far East (standard products, and labor-intensive assembly), in a way that makes the whole system stronger. But this intelligence is not all that makes this company special – cutting-edge technology innovation has made this small company one of the world market leaders in microbatteries (delivering, for example, to Apple as well as hearing aid companies), and a charismatic leader has energized the organization to contribute to innovation from multiple sources.

5.1 Introduction

"A company is like a volleyball team: everyone knows what everyone has to do; it's about 'smelling' where the ball is coming from. If you lose, the coach loses. If you win, the team wins." In the 15 years that Dr. Dejan Ilic has been with Varta Microbattery GmbH, for nine of those years as CEO, the company has grown from a DM8 million to €50 million business. Ilic is clear about the reasons for this success: "If you want to build a future you have to learn from the past – and you need innovation in every area, otherwise there will be no future. At Varta Microbattery, everything is always in development, including management – we need innovation at all levels. We put one new product (not a modification, an entirely new product) into development every year and each new product requires a new technology. We also bring three to five new products to market every year. Our technical people give solutions to customers, but innovation is also necessary in sales and marketing."

Acknowledged as a market and technology leader in the rechargeable microbattery and hearing aid battery sectors, and 6 years after being spun off from its parent company VARTA AG, Varta Microbattery (VM) has become a multi-award winning company that has proved it can survive in Europe at a time when both blue- and white-collar jobs in the sector are increasingly being moved offshore. In April 2006, VM won INSEAD's prestigious Industrial Excellence Award for Germany, and in January 2007, the company was awarded a new prize by the German government for being the best innovator in German business.

How has VM done this? By combining world-class innovation with finding the right balance between off-shoring and in-shoring, which means locating operations where it makes the most business sense for the company and for their European and Asian markets. Refusing to adopt a one-size-fits-all mentality, VM invents and produces unique innovative high-tech products in Germany while offshoring other production operations to China and Indonesia, keeping its overall labor costs low – a business model that bucks the trend for the sector.

VM's fundamental business principle is to produce in Germany, and deliver in Asia. While products like single cell batteries, designed for hearing aids and other similar products, are manufactured in Germany and distributed direct to customers, the high-profile original equipment manufacturer (OEM) products are developed in Germany and completed and packaged in Asia. As Dr. Ilic puts it, "Imagine we make a jacket – we make the body in Germany, and add the left arm and zipper in Asia." The major factor here is the influence of labor cost on total production cost. Dr. Ilic maintains that labor cost must stay at around 10–15%: "If it goes much higher, you're dead." In Germany, this is achieved through automation and reliability. Although automation implies a high investment, and the product itself is the result of expensive, leading edge R&D and technology, this leads to reduced labor costs. In Asia, where assembly and packaging work is done, the labor costs are much cheaper and the technical demands less critical.

As a result the company's make up has changed since VM spun off from the parent company in 2001. At that time, the company's activities could be broken down as 50% sales, 30% manufacturing and 20% technical development. Five years later, the breakdown is 80% technical and manufacturing and 20% sales operations.

For such a flexible, entrepreneurial company to emerge from a business more than 100 years old has required a culture change across the entire workforce, a focus on innovation throughout all the company's products, systems and functions.

5.2 Background

VARTA batteries have played a part in some of mankind's most significant advances over the last 120 years, including Nansen's first polar expedition in the 1890s, and the Apollo 11 moon landing in 1969. The company started in Germany in 1888 as Busche and Müller. By 1904, and following investments by AEG and Siemens, the company was established as VARTA, which stood for *Vertrieb* (sales), *Aufladung* (charging) *Reparatur* (repair) *transportabler* (transportable) *Akkumulatoren* (storage batteries). VARTA always sought to be at the forefront of power technology – the first US cars sold in Germany were powered by VARTA batteries, the batteries Nansen took to the North Pole were designed to withstand temperatures of −50°C, the company that produced the first storable dry-cell batteries was acquired in 1926, and 23 patents were granted in 1955 for VARTA's paper-lined battery and dry-cell separator, the prelude to mass production. By 1962, all car batteries were marketed under the Varta name, which was recognized internationally as a benchmark for quality and high performance.

VARTA set up its first overseas production plant in Singapore in 1972, and its first sales office in Hong Kong in 1975. By 1977, it was clear that VARTA was several different things, and the company split into three to focus resources on the automotive, portable and consumer battery sectors. International expansion continued over the next decade and a half, and an assembly plant was established in Batam, Indonesia in 1991. Button cell manufacturing was created as a business line by Dr. Dejan Ilic at the beginning of the 1990s. The unit was transferred to Ellwangen, Germany, in 1997 so that production could be fully automated.

VARTA Microbatterie GmbH, the spin-off from Ilic's unit, was set up in 2001 to focus on new miniature battery technologies, especially products designed for OEMs in the mobile communication, medical and electronic equipment markets. In the same year, a joint-venture plant was set up in Guangzhou to meet the growing demand for microbatteries in China. The year 2002 saw VARTA's portable battery division merge with the US company Rayovac. The automotive division was sold to another American company, Johnson Controls Inc. VARTA Microbattery GmbH (VM) was established as an independent company. Five years later, VM's success in finding solutions to both their customers' technical problems and the challenge of optimizing production costs made the company the market leader in notebook computers, engineering applications and electronic steering modules, and second in medical applications and hearing aids.

VM's consumer products are marketed under the PowerOne brand, while VARTA-branded batteries are marketed to OEM customers. PowerOne encompasses a wide range of microbattery technologies, including zinc–air, rechargeable Ni–MH, lithium, silver oxide, alkaline manganese and the new PoLiFlex, an innovative polymer battery that has no free liquid electrolyte, so is highly safe with no risk of leakage. PowerOne batteries are used in, among other things, hearing aids, photographic equipment, computers, smart cards and small electronic, portable and medical devices. Thin film batteries and micro fuel cells are being developed for several applications (see Figs. 5.1 and 5.2). The company has around 1,300 staff worldwide and in 2005 supplied over 400 million microbatteries, with sales amounting to around €130 million.

5.3 New Thinking

The traditional value model for VARTA was based on the technology, projected size of the company, cost-based controls, and a focus on matching the expectations of the German shareholders. The new thinking at VM stresses profitability, linking advances in technology directly to profit, introducing value-based control and an orientation towards international capital markets.

The motto for today's market positioning is "Mobility for you," for both customers and business partners worldwide. This translates into technology development priorities. In addition, VM's business strategy is to remain entrepreneurial and innovation-driven within the company, making sure that R&D is fully integrated with customer needs – building on the simple assumption that innovations that do not address customer needs will not be profitable.

Gas Sensor   30GB Photo Storage Viewer

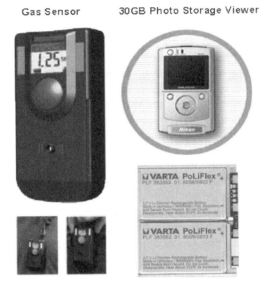

Fig. 5.1. Varta microbatteries for electronic devices

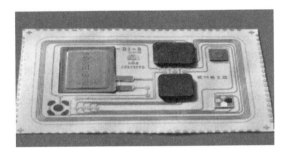

Fig. 5.2. Thin film battery for multi-sensor card

VM keeps a weather eye on the market, and aims to create concrete connections between actions, the competitive environment and growth. Identifying key competitive advantages and making sure that they are recognized by employees is an important part of translating strategy into functions. For example, the internal emphasis on quality and reliability demonstrably confers an advantage, as does the company's emphasis on innovation in all areas, from specific products, innovative systems, and even the part played by the company's award-winning package design. However, the focus, at all levels of the organization, is on providing customer solutions, from the production of a new high capacity cell for hearing aids, to a system for speeding up supply to market.

Six over-riding values guide and orientate VM employees – results, customers, quality, teamwork, innovation and integrity. Among VM's many awards are Innovator of the Year 2004 and Entrepreneur of the Year 2005 (for Ilic), honors that indicate how successful Varta has been in translating its values, strategies and goals into tangible results.

Many companies claim to be entrepreneurial, open to innovation and focused on customer needs, but few live up to their claims. VM is one of those that do. What are the driving forces behind the culture change that has enabled the company to achieve so spectacularly in such a short space of time?

5.4 Charisma, Culture Change and Team Building

Dr. Dejan Ilic does not like the word "motivation." He prefers to talk about mobilization: "There's an Einstein in everyone; you just need to wake him up. No one [at VM] has a big job description. I never ask, 'What do you want to do?' The right questions are, 'Where do you want to work? Where can you exploit your performance in the best way?'" When Ilic became CEO of VM in 1998, he had already built a reputation for his entrepreneurial approach within the parent company. He began his career as a researcher into rechargeable energy storage, and in 1996, as part of VARTA AG's management team, set up round cell battery production facilities at Ellwangen. As VM spun off from VARTA AG, a creative leader was needed, someone who would infuse entrepreneurial principles into the organization, add value, and develop innovative ideas to beat competitors. The CEO would have to understand employee needs and provide a framework for them to align their aspirations with the vision of the company. Dejan Ilic was the obvious choice.

Tall, physically imposing, with immense energy and a beguiling sense of humor, Ilic is unexpectedly approachable. A passionate sportsman and former national youth player for the Serbian volleyball team, he founded a junior volleyball team when he first moved to Ellwangen and ever since has been a prominent figure in the local community. At VM, he is a figure of respect and admiration – but not deference – and a point of reference for everyone ("As Dr. Ilic says…").

Arno Perner, General Manager R&D, summarizes Ilic's style as a leader: "He believes in developing people – team building, forming creative clusters: he identifies good young people, gives them early opportunities and brings them on. Everyone is responsibilized at all levels of the company. There's a sense of ownership – acknowledgement of performance and achievement. There's a process whereby people can bring their own ideas to improve processes and products. Ideas are rewarded – not just financially, but also through prizes and recognition." At the same time, teamwork and cross-functional collaboration (see Sect. 5) prevent such individual rewards from making people selfish in the way they offer their ideas.

Asked how the VM leader accomplishes this, Dr. Perner replies, with no hesitation: "He changed the philosophy of the company and was creative from the beginning. His major advantage is as a team builder and motivator. Perhaps his greatest gift is bringing people and skills together – he makes people do things they didn't realize they could do."

Dr. Perner knows this better than most. He was 13, and a half-hearted high school student, when he first met Ilic, who coached him as a member of Ellwangen's junior volleyball team, which has proven to be a rich training ground for more than volleyball players. Perner became Ilic's protégé, working at VM as an intern for 20 h a week while he was at university, and eventually graduating as the top chemistry student in Germany. At Ilic's suggestion, Perner studied for his doctorate at the University of Ulm, where Ilic recommended a specific supervisor. VM sponsored Perner's PhD, with no obligation for him to join Varta on completion. Perner has never worked anywhere else.

Dr. Perner's story is not unique. VM take at least three students on internships every year, with the intake coming from European universities, notably local institutes, like the University of Ulm and the nearest Fraunhofer Institute, and the University of Graz in Austria. Interns usually go into production, technology or R&D. Like Perner, they have no contract and they are not obliged to stay in the company while they are sponsored for their degrees. Significantly, however, all these interns remain with the company. Staff turnover is very low and new recruits from outside the company are almost invariably young: it is very unusual for more mature people to join.

Dejan Ilic probably deserves the epithet "charismatic" more than most CEOs who would like to be thought so. While he expects a great deal from VM personnel, he begins from a very humane basis: "You have to trust people and if people need support you have to provide it. I talk to everyone, they all talk to me. You have to allow people the flexibility to make mistakes. I say to them, 'You can make a mistake; but you can't make the same mistake twice.' In 15 years I have only fired two people. Sometimes people do not want to take responsibility and if that happens, you have to find a way to take out the fear."

5.5 "Innovations in Every Field and Every Day"

It is no accident that VM is thriving in Swabia, a European center of excellence for medium-sized engineering companies, with a high concentration of specialized technical manufacturers. In a country where there is 10% unemployment nationwide, Swabia has less than 5%. Even though VM's production facilities require some of the most sophisticated and cutting-edge instrument design and supply available today, many of these resources are within a radius of tens of kilometers from Ellwangen.

Of the 500 employees in Ellwangen, 150 (a high proportion) work in R&D as engineers, technicians and designers. New product developers work with design engineers from the conceptual stage of every project. Projects are evaluated in a feasibility study in which production, marketing and R&D participate equally. About 20% of projects get past the feasibility study stage. Resources are divided almost equally between short- and long-term projects, with slightly more being devoted to the latter. Project teams are small, usually between four and eight people, with most people working on two or three different projects, and project managers generally oversee one major and two smaller projects. New technology projects tend to have a 2-year life span; shorter projects may last 6 months. Regular meetings with sales, marketing, logistics, R&D and quality control monitor product development and progress. These are held monthly for the single-cell, direct-to-consumer products, fortnightly for OEM products – schedules are vital, because products are developed to market times.

Nevertheless, R&D time is considered an essential, not a luxury. "People need time to be creative, we have to let them have crazy ideas," says Arno Perner. He cites an example where research into a process using lasers for welding proved a non-starter but unexpectedly revolutionized production in another way. "Our laser specialists realized that the lasers could be adapted to another process and used for cutting instead of welding. We were producing a wide range of electrodes and each one needed new, customized stainless steel cutting tools to be developed. A stainless steel tool needed 3 months' manufacturing time, whereas the laser cutter could be reprogrammed in 3 h and adapted to each individual electrode. The cost and time advantages were enormous."

Innovation at VM means more than new technology. Production time and costs have a significant impact on profits and VM constantly reviews production and processes to ensure that maximum throughput is obtained. When opportunities for improvements in production are spotted, operators are asked for their input and suggestions, in some cases playing as great a role as the engineers in developing modifications. In general, VM aims to action items within a month, although this time frame varies depending on the nature of the implementation. A minor adjustment might be in place within 4–6 weeks, while a major change will be implemented more speedily, within 2–3 weeks. Two teams look at continuous process optimization (quality, cost reduction and product improvement): a cost reduction team, with members drawn from R&D, production and quality control, and a quality control/production team. Both teams meet at least once a month: input is roughly 70% from engineers, 20–30% from operators. Additionally, people from the production line are invited to give information, input and present ideas about improvements to these committees. One result of team consultation was efforts to reduce bottlenecks and improve changeovers on one production line, which raised output from 15,000 to 21,000 units per day, an increase of 40%.

Supply systems are another area where VM's innovative approach has helped streamline and improve the economics of the process. VM's supply chain has to work over thousands of kilometers, and for the OEM products, where production aims for just-in-time delivery, it is critical to the company's success. Working to market speed, VM has developed what Logistics Manager Jürgen Schwenk describes as a "luxury situation" where volumes out and volumes in are balanced. Three times a week, fixed allotments of basic cells are supplied to the Asian assembly plants by air – and finished products are brought back the same way, rather than by cheaper but lengthy ocean freight. VM profits from the fact that eastbound to Asia, planes have a huge amount of capacity available, which forces transport prices down. Enormous quantities of finished product come out of China so there is a lot of cheap empty space going back there. It costs the same to fly one kilogram of goods to Shanghai as it does to move one kilogram from Ellwangen to France.

Of the bare battery cells sent out from Ellwangen to its Asian plants, 50% will be expected back in Europe in the form of finished product, while 50% goes to Asian markets. VM has tripartite agreements with airlines and forwarders that allow it to secure air freight when customer demand peaks. This is crucial for OEM supplies, which are market driven. With these flexible freight arrangements, VM can adjust quantities right up to the last minute, both east-west and west-east.

5.6 Innovation Supported by Off-Shoring and In-Shoring

German companies face a number of issues when considering off-shoring operations. Germany has had high unemployment since reunification, and the creation of new jobs is slow. Labor laws not only make it difficult to lay off workers, but also make the process of creating new job categories, and hiring workers to fill them, lengthy and bureaucratic. But off-shoring can help companies to be more flexible and better able to meet fluctuating demand for their products, a key driver of profits for manufacturing companies.

Off-shoring has been a part of VARTA's business strategy for over 30 years, not only to minimize production costs, but also to ensure that the company can service its global customers effectively. However, as well as off-shoring, VARTA has not been slow to bring work back to Germany – in-shoring – when it has made the most business sense. For example, VARTA AG brought parts of the production process back to Germany from Singapore in the late 1990s, which helped the company to overcome delivery and quality problems and also to benefit from a more skilled workforce. The result was greater efficiencies and a 15% reduction in wage costs associated with production.

VM is the biggest employer in Ellwangen and plays a major role in the local economy. The off-shoring of assembly jobs, driven by the increase in high-cost development jobs, initially created union problems. However, overall, jobs in Ellwangen increased. The regular staff of 500 is usually augmented by 50–55 temporary staff from around the world; worldwide, VM employs 1,300. Streamlining off-shoring also meant job losses overseas. In the 1990s, there were a huge number of assembly services worldwide. VM created know-how design and technology centers, eliminated small assembly plants and concentrated the assembly of core products on Batam Island. Now, all the engineering expertise is sourced from Ellwangen. People from there go to Asia for 2–3 weeks to train people on site; every year, between five and ten Asian workers come to Ellwangen to train for a similar length of time. However, changes in the complexity of end products mean that knowledge and expertise are no longer the preserve of Ellwangen's engineers. While many are standard, routine products, other new products, such as the new lithium polymer batteries, require significant amounts of knowledge in Asia. The new products require more know-how and skills on the shop floor, and in terms of quality control, than 5 years ago. Increasingly, Asian personnel must be at the same level as their colleagues in Germany, and highly trained. To ensure this, Varta arranges regular worldwide workshops and engineers travel frequently to Asia to maintain levels of expertise and training.

In Ellwangen, VM has focused on establishing and maintaining high-value, highly skilled jobs and cost-effective automated production lines. The plant there is responsible for meeting global cell battery demand, and supplies packed single cells directly to markets. PowerOne batteries are marketed direct to consumers, including professionals. VM grew its market share in this sector from 16% in 2004 to 25% in 2006.

Technology innovation in PowerOne batteries focuses not only on the batteries themselves – durability and reliability – but also on packaging and ease of insertion of the battery into the device. Recent innovations have included the development of a single cell with the highest capacity yet achieved (an increase of 10% on the previous best), and the development of chemistry to produce rechargeable hearing aid batteries, the first in the world.

A core assortment of single cells (e.g., mobile phone batteries), produced on highly automated lines, form the basis of customized battery solutions for OEMs. Multiple and diverse kinds of chemistry are involved in the development of a wide range of systems. Ellwangen scientists identify the chemistry needed for each application and design the electro-chemistry of each specialized cell. All cell assembly work, testing and sampling, is done by technicians and engineers in Ellwangen. The cells are then sent to plants in Batam, Shanghai and Guangzhou where the plastic and electronic components are added. This is labor-intensive but routine work, involving tiny, complicated parts.

Original equipment manufacturers are very important customers for VM. VARTA batteries are found in a range of mobile devices, including laptop computers, mobile phones and the Apple iPod. VM has a worldwide sales network, and provides global sales support and logistics, so its customers deal directly with the company rather than with distributors. For customers whose operations are also global, such as Apple, with headquarters in California and production in China, this means that VM is on the doorstep in both locations.

VM's Chinese and Indonesian plants are wholly owned by the company and are run as individual profit centers. The first was opened in Shanghai in 1998, driven by VM's major client at the time, Siemens mobile phones, and all now work on assembly of a variety of portable consumer items, mainly MP3 devices, mobile phones, and the Apple iPod. The Shanghai plant is owned by Varta Singapore and managed from there. Singapore is used as a distribution hub for consumer goods assembled and finished in Asia.

All the offshore plants are managed by local nationals. This is consistent with Ilic's policy of recruiting management, sales and marketing people from the country in which they operate. Although there is a high level of international job rotation, management by local nationals is seen as essential to the transfer of know-how and country market specifics. With up to four new products coming to market every year, and refinements constantly being made to existing products, training in the assembly of complex OEM products is a continual operation. People are sent out from Ellwangen to Shanghai to train assembly workers on the spot. This is usually a 2- to 3-year secondment, supported by a quality manager in the overseas plants. It is not unusual for managers to undertake more than one overseas assignment. Juergen Schwenk, VM Logistics Manager now based in Ellwangen, spent 3 years in logistics in the United States and 3 years in Asia, becoming familiar with local production facilities, market specifics and suppliers.

OEM product meetings are held fortnightly, grouping sales, marketing, logistics, R&D and quality control. Market demand, and flexibility to meet fluctuations in it, are monitored constantly, so that VM is always prepared for a swift response to changing conditions in consumer behavior – Dejan Ilic observes, "We have a responsibility for our customers' customers." With logistics tied closely to sales and marketing, there is an in-built agility in the supply system. Timing is critical. Factories in Ellwangen and Indonesia are monitored by product management in Germany. Two systems are used to steer product capacity. The highly automated production lines in Ellwangen produce 15–20 types of bare button cells, not finished products. Because time delays are introduced every time the equipment has to be changed to produce a specific type of cell, engineers aim to keep the machines running for as long as possible. This goes against the principle of avoiding keeping a large amount of inventory, so only a limited number of items are stored in Ellwangen. Bare cells are flown out and stocked in Asian factories. The high speed production in Ellwangen is customer forecast driven; the bare cells produced there are used to produce 1,500–2,000 different articles in Asia. The flexibility is in the Asian plants. There can be an overnight response to customer demands in production in Asia, with lead times of 2 weeks out of Singapore (the distribution centre) and 1-week transportation.

The direct sales force and sales engineers collaborate closely with OEM product development teams to understand their problems and how best to solve them. Systematic and frequent customer surveys are carried out, directly and via country websites in the local language. Responses are analyzed and acted upon. Additional websites for OEM customers provide extra technical data. With this attention to detail, VM can customize its OEM products from conception to delivery – from the product itself to the packaging that is used for it. As Ilic recognizes, "The smaller things make people happy."

5.7 And the Future?

VARTA Microbatterie GmbH is a small company that gives the impression that there is a reactive core of perpetual energy hidden somewhere deep inside it. With concentrated, local provisions, it produces world-leading technology and bio-chemistry, and highly specialized, cutting-edge products. It does this not only by producing where it makes most sense, economically and logistically, but also by recognizing and rewarding innovation as part of the company's culture just as much as an indispensable aspect of the business in which company is involved. This is the result of charismatic leadership, supported by a stable, long-serving manage-ment and workforce, which fosters a creative and compelling work environment.

In late 2006, Varta Microbatterie was put up for sale by its owner. Ilic assembled a group of interested investors and made an offer in the spirit of a management buyout. His investor group was outbid by a rival investor group. In 2007, Varta made record profits. However, the test of sustainability under new management has yet to be passed. It will be interesting to see what Varta Microbatteries becomes over the next few years.

In general, short-term profitability is easy to achieve in a sound company that has developed a solid position of innovation leadership. We have seen situations where companies have achieved it by cutting R&D expenses and selling and leas-ing back real estate. In this book we want to emphasize that competitive advantage rests on sound management, which identifies an advantageous strategic position, mobilizes employees to contribute to the height of their abilities, and orchestrates them into a system that is more than the sum of its parts. The obvious implication of this is that the competitive position can easily unravel through short-term or financial-only management.[1]

---

[1] Sources: Company visits and interviews; presentation by Dr. Dejan Ilic; *Financial Times*, May 29, 2001, August 6, 2002, August 7, 2002.

Chapter 6

Hewlett Packard Herrenberg: Partnership Solutions*

This chapter describes the journey Hewlett Packard's large computer systems production organization took from lean production, through distribution effectiveness, to flexibility. All of these principles were useful but not sufficient to track successfully the increase in competitive intensity in the industry. The latest step was a change to a solution factory, where computers were combined with services, in a partner network, in which HP itself performed only a small part of the set of activities. The partner concept helped the company to take the last successful step to sustained profitability.

6.1 Introduction

Bill Hewlett and Dave Packard famously founded their eponymous company in a California garage in 1939, deciding whose name went first with the toss of a coin. The first commercial product was an audio oscillator, which the two electrical engineers sold to Walt Disney Studios. HP opened its first manufacturing plant outside the US in Germany in 1959 and today the company operates in more than 170 countries around the world, offering a wide range of computing and imaging solutions and services for business and home consumers. Since merging with Compaq in early 2002, HP has become market leader in most of its business segments. Revenues for the year to July 2006 topped $90 billion, with 60% coming from sales outside the US.

The company has never stood still. New technologies have been a regular feature of HP's growth, from the early radio frequency equipment to the latest in printing innovation. HP introduced the first personal computer, then called a "desk-top scientific calculator," in 1968. It introduced the first calculator to print Japanese characters in 1973 and the world's brightest LED in 1994. But HP is not just about new technology; it has also led the way in workplace design and management. In 1942, HP built an open-plan office building, designed for versatility and to spark creativity by encouraging communication between workers. HP was the first company to introduce flexitime in the US, and Bill Hewlett and Dave Packard's strong belief in talking regularly with their staff was the original "management by walking around" (MBWA).

---

* This chapter was written by Hendrik Brumme (University of Reutlingen) and Luk N. Van Wassenhove (INSEAD).

Not surprisingly, then, HP constantly strives for improvement and ways to serve its customers better. Two major challenges for IT manufacturers nowadays are product standardization and commoditization, which creates cost pressures, and the rapidly increasing demand for customized solutions. HP's printer and PC operations adopted the "no asset" supply chain very early, placing a strategic focus on outsourcing and off-shoring most operational functions. HP's enterprise business, including HP in Germany, took a slightly different approach, and this chapter looks at how HP's German operations developed a business model that can cope with today's demanding market.

The German factory is located in Herrenberg, near Stuttgart, and produces HP's UNIX servers, mass storage products and workstations, offering 3,500 different products from low-end servers to high-end scalable systems. These products are configured to order and there are more than 10,000 options, resulting in millions of possible product combinations. Eighty percent of the orders have to be manufactured within 24 h. Annual revenues are nearly \$2.5 billion, but daily product demand can vary widely, from \$0.5 million to \$16 million a day.

To meet this kind of demand, HP Germany had to develop an innovative supply structure and in the process created a new, industry-leading fulfillment model. The model was developed in four phases, starting in the early 1990s. In Phase 1, the focus was on developing manufacturing processes that could cope with producing constantly evolving products. Phase 2, the Distribution Centre, dealt with operational excellence and cost competitiveness. Here we look at Phase 3, the Velocity Factory, and Phase 4, the Solution Factory, which have culminated in the Partner Park concept.

The Velocity Factory was HP's response to the rising threat of cheaper labor in other European countries. Flexible processes, new workforce models and more efficient approaches to asset management were needed if HP Germany was to remain competitive.

Phase 4 saw HP Germany adopt a new strategic focus – to take over the integration activities that were frequently provided by outside companies, such as independent software vendors (ISVs), and so build complex plug and play solutions for its customers from start to finish. Solution integration requires many skills, and the stroke of genius for HP was to acquire these skills without costly investment. Different supply chain partners with complementary skills were physically moved into the factory, creating an integrated value collaboration network. This permitted skills and capabilities to be bundled and enhanced so that both partners and HP gained customers and increased revenues. The HP Partner Park was born.

Figure 6.1 demonstrates the reduction in manufacturing depth and the move towards services and value collaboration with business partners over time.

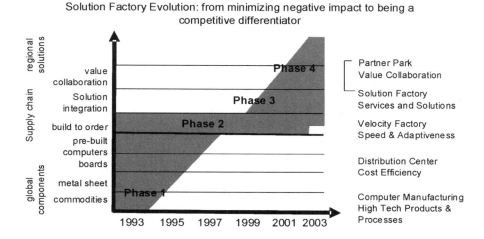

Fig. 6.1. The evolution of HP Herrenberg's capabilities

6.2 The Velocity Factory Concept

Coping with extreme business volatility requires flexibility to match. Manufacturers must avoid the costs associated with carrying excess inventory and obsolescence, while at the same time ensuring that they do not lose sales or customers through failing to meet their requirements. In 1998, HP conceptualized the Velocity Factory. The major goals of the Velocity Factory were speed, flexibility and lowest possible cost. To meet these goals, HP's management adopted the best practices of an apparently distinct industry – food and groceries. Their insight was that high-tech equipment could be equated to fresh merchandise, such as fruit and vegetables, where perishable products must be processed and sold quickly.

The first step in designing the Velocity Factory was to disaggregate the product architecture into modular systems and to use the concept of late differentiation. Pre-assembled kits called lowest common denominator (LCD) were obtained from HP facilities located in tax and salary havens. Orders for unique parts were consolidated by the purchasing system at a global level and forwarded to suppliers, with deliveries split by region in order to gain economies of scale in purchasing.

The second element was to execute manufacturing processes in parallel. A customer order was broken down into independent work objects such as computers, disk drives, software products and accessories. The work objects document listed all the parts required to complete the order, when and where the parts were needed, when assembly had to begin and the deadline for shipment.

The third component was a flexible workforce structure. Compensating for the higher labor costs in Germany meant establishing a workforce model that was flexible enough to deal with huge variations in demand while keeping productivity above 85%. The flexible workforce structure had four distinct groups of workers. The first were permanent HP staff, also known as "solution experts." Solution experts accounted for 14% of the workforce and made up its core – they were the ones who kept the know-how within HP. The second group was HP temporary staff, and provided monthly flexibility. HP temporary staff accounted for 9% of the workforce and could be hired and fired on a monthly basis. The third group as external temporary staff, and provided weekly flexibility. They accounted for about 10% of the workforce on average and could be hired and fired on a weekly basis. The remaining workforce came from contract manufacturers located in HP's manufacturing facility. The overlaying component was the work–time model, which provided daily and hourly flexibility, for HP staff and also for partners and service providers. Workers had an individual flex account that kept track of the number of hours worked, and each worker was trained on an average of five different types of job. The workday was split into four blocks, with a maximum possible work time of 10 h per block. At short notice, the workers had to show up any time within the pre-assigned block and they could be told to stop work and go home at any time.

HP outsourced its processes extensively, and located strategic partners within the HP factory to develop the IT infrastructure and enterprise resource planning system. Extensive outsourcing shifted the business environment from an internally integrated supply chain to a complex network of contract manufacturers, third-party logistics providers, and suppliers, with HP as the orchestrator.

The redesign produced significant benefits. The raw material inventory dropped by more than 50%. On-time delivery performance improved to more than 98%, while order fulfillment time dropped to 2 days on average. Factory capacity could be increased by 400% within 24 h when there was a sudden increase in demand. The work–time model saved 17% compared to traditional worker deployment methods. Finally, the total spend on manufacturing and administrative expenses, including all subcontracting activities, dropped by 50% in 2001.

6.3 The Way Ahead: The Solution Factory Concept

The lack of opportunities to differentiate product offerings puts significant pressure on margins in this industry. Hardware is only useful when it is integrated with other hardware and software applications, and these could come from HP or from third-party ISVs. Most integration activities were done outside HP, at partners' or customers' premises. In Phase 4, management at HP Germany recognized that customers who ordered configure-to-order computers wanted not only a computer but a whole solution, including application software, optimized and ready to run.

Large customers also asked for specific customized product portfolios and supply chain collaboration. So having rolled out the Velocity Factory design, HP Germany turned to developing a new approach that would better satisfy its customers. The new business model was called the Solution Factory, and the basic ideas behind the new model were to:

- Increase the value-added offered by the factory with product/services hybrids, customization, and even complex solutions shipped directly to end-users
- Shift standard manufacturing activities to a lower cost point in the value chain
- Leverage existing infrastructure from mainstream business by combining standard processes (as modules) to build individual solutions
- Support sales through customer collaboration, plug-and-play solutions and by offering best practice events with customers and partners in the factory

Through the Solution Factory, HP had to develop a portfolio of service offerings that would allow it to provide plug-and-play solutions directly from the factory to end-users. The company had to go beyond its build-to-customer-order model and offer customized, ready-to-go solutions using volume manufacturing processes (mass customization). Some of its solutions included procurement of third-party components (sometimes competitors' products, if that was what the customer wanted), customized labeling, installation of specific software applications and pre-integration.

The Solution Factory would also have to assume a new role within HP, working very closely with the sales organization. As part of this initiative, HP opened up its factory to customers so that they could see how their solutions were being built, and at the same time share best practice and provide training for the customers' engineers. This tactic acted as a key market differentiator, because visiting the factory gave customers greater confidence in HP's ability to meet their requirements.

Figure 6.2 shows the shift from velocity to solutions and the four key areas that had to be developed. Operational excellence was still the core responsibility of the Solution Factory. To increase the range of solutions offered, partners who could provide specific know-how and capabilities were needed, and skills had to be developed to link and unlink those partners quickly.

The new service capabilities ultimately allowed HP to serve different types of customers according to their individual needs, and put the Solution Factory into a position to be a tool for sales and an essential partner for HP's customers.

The Solution Factory's service offerings were based on four building blocks:

- Start-up services: these included configuration, integration, installation of operating system (custom software), testing and shipping the entire solution in one shipment to a customer site. These solutions were ready to operate, requiring minimum start-up time.

- Original equipment manufacturer (OEM)/independent software vendor (ISV) catalogue solutions: HP provided a variety of ready-to-go solutions under these services, including order fulfillment, procurement, customer-specific application loading, product life cycle management, customized labeling and boxing, and relationship management.
- Complex solutions: these one-off solutions were managed like a project. HP nominated an overall project leader – also known as the single point of contact at the factory – who organized everything related to the delivery of the solution.
- Supply chain services: HP provided a range of supply chain services, including procurement, distribution, and consulting. This most important service enabled HP's supply chain staff to link with external customers and build a common supply chain.

HP Solution Factory

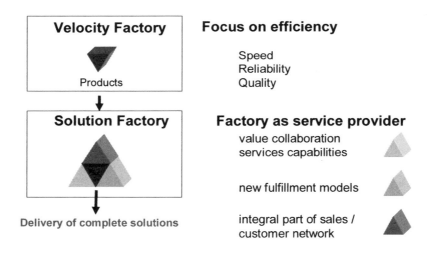

Fig. 6.2. Development dimensions of the solution factory

The Solution Factory was a network of different organizations with complementary capabilities. Not only were different CMs for operations services integrated, but engineering partners provided change-related services to deal with the volatility in volume and capabilities. HP modularized some of the engineering work and outsourced it to a third-party service provider whenever the volume of orders reached critical levels. Upstream, HP's customer-facing organizations used the Solution Factory to complement their own service offerings, which could potentially bring new business to the Solution Factory.

Three principles for cooperation had to be developed to make the Solution Factory work: first, a formalized system of communication; second, a clearly agreed service portfolio with well-defined prices and related roles and responsibilities; and third, access to the factory resources for all partners. The overall objective of the collaboration was to leverage the complementary capabilities of each partner to the fullest extent.

6.4 HP Partner Park: A Business Network Concept

6.4.1 Why Further Change?

Two major trends impacted the factory significantly. First, the trend toward product standardization and commoditization, and second, the need to simplify the buying process for customers and give them the applications they wanted in a world of increasingly complex products. Customers wanted tailored solutions, on time and fast, while shareholders expected the cost structures associated with the volume consumer industry. Increasing competition and a growing over-capacity in the market placed enormous cost pressures on the supply chain. At the same time, increasing CM capabilities and global opportunities gave HP new possibilities for constructing the entire enterprise supply chain.

HP Germany was also threatened by the possibility that solutions might be shipped directly from the HP factory in Singapore, leaving HP Germany to provide only local administration support. They were going to have to compete on more than excellence in distribution. Cost sensitive and standardized products were being moved offshore and the local factories had to start focusing on customized solutions.

In the Velocity Factory phase, collaboration was focused on inbound vendors and service providers (outsourcing). Money and time were still wasted when it came to HP's outbound supply chain. Channel partners, OEMs, system integrators (SIs) and ISVs bought HP computer equipment and then added further value using their own integration and configuration centers.

With the Solution Factory concept, HP pursued a one-touch direct shipment model. Customer orders from HP salespeople or from external sales partners would be routed into the factory, built and integrated, and then shipped directly to the end-customer. This new delivery approach raised questions about some of the value add of HP's distributors, namely local market scanning, sales and especially fulfillment. Partners still played an important role in business generation, but no longer contributed logistics services. Partner integration centers tended to be located close to the HP factories, so did not provide any geographical advantages. They produced lower volumes compared to the HP factory, which resulted in adversarial learning curves, and had limited solution integration capabilities, with view automation only. In addition, overcapacity and infrastructure duplications increased total supply chain cost.

So HP explored how this part of the supply chain could be integrated into one common value network to reduce costs further. When developing this, the perspective was broadened to consider how to get closer to the customer in order to capture maximum profit from the customer's total cost of ownership, while at the same time keeping that cost of ownership as low as possible, both in terms of money and hassle. HP managers asked themselves if the HP supply chain could be cost efficient *and* enable revenue generation.

6.4.2 The Partner Park Idea

HP's idea was to develop an end-to-end delivery model that enabled the company and its business partners to act as a single, virtual delivery and value chain. The competences and capabilities of all partners in the Partner Park would be increased if they collaborated in selling and delivering a broader set of HP solutions and IT infrastructures, leading to corporate growth all around.

Thus, the Partner Park was a further development from the "all under one roof" concept used to create the Velocity Factory – now HP was talking about a "center of gravitation." The factory was reconfigured to be part of a closed loop supply chain. With its complete infrastructure designed for mass-customization and linked to service providers and logistic forwarders, the factory would be the central hub for all kinds of physical integration, from final assembly to complex industry solutions.

The plan was to bring in partners with complementary skills to enhance capabilities through the whole business network, to share data and information without too many formal processes, to leverage the existing infrastructure between the partners, and to share inventory both upstream and downstream (Fig. 6.3).

All partners would keep their legal independence and business autonomy; however, the Partner Park should look and feel like one common operation. The partner owning a particular deal would then act as an orchestrator coordinating the other Partner Park partners and processes.

Moving from the Solution Factory to the Partner Park required three important changes to the existing set-up. The first step was for HP to get its channel partners – resellers, distributors and value added service providers – to collaborate and to think about moving their integration centers into the HP factory buildings. The channel partners would also be able to use HP's infrastructure at the factory, or access it remotely, in order to modify or customize a product when HP did not have the necessary expertise, and then HP would deliver the product to the end customer. The partners would also be able to work with HP engineers in problem-solving teams. Each partner within the value collaboration network would focus on their own area of expertise. A well-defined service portfolio was needed, listing all possible collaboration activities and their corresponding prices.

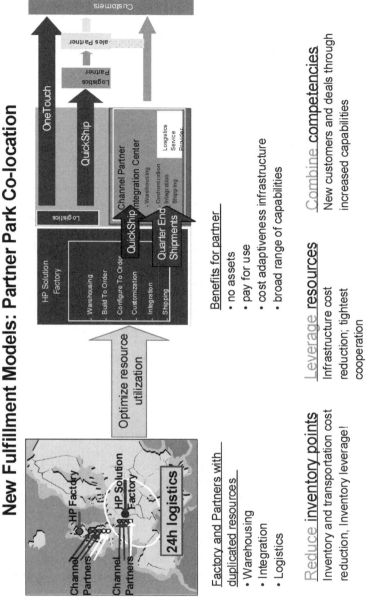

Fig. 6.3. Moving channel partners' integration activities into the Partner Park

All the physical product and order fulfillment would be done in the Solution Factory, to gain leverage and efficiency in the supply chain. Doing all the integration work at a single place would eliminate duplication, be faster and guarantee quality.

6.4.3 Partner Park Results and Benefits

Material and information flows within the Partner Park are very short and flexible. The co-location has created new possibilities for intensifying cooperation between HP and its channel partners, with the physical closeness of employees from these different companies simplifying communication and cooperation. The end result has helped to grow the business.

Set-up costs were low, and mostly limited to linking IT systems so that orders and financial data could be transferred. Within 6 months, it was possible to demonstrate not only the operational effectiveness but also the efficiency of the new arrangement. Fulfillment costs fell by 15% for the distribution partners and overall revenues increased by 25%, because distributors could now offer services delivered by the network. The number of new customers increased, and it became possible to leverage inventory, which increased availability while lowering the inventory level. Data and information sharing were not only limited to formal communication processes. The employees of the different companies met informally every day and exchanged valuable information. Marketing campaigns were communicated early and forecasts developed together.

End customers were served with complete solutions, much faster and more efficiently than ever before. All partners were now able to offer a much broader service portfolio without augmenting the infrastructure cost, which increased revenue generation. Different nodes in the outbound supply chain were eliminated and consolidated under the roof of the Solution Factory. Partner Park became a real one-stop shop, delivering computer hardware, services and complex IT infrastructure solutions.

6.5 Management Implications

Value networks are an important and powerful weapon when an industry's products move into a mature phase. They enable the supply chain to offer a greater range of products and services, and to offer customized solutions at lower cost. Fundamentally important is that partners offer complementary skills, to prevent competition and to enlarge the service offering of the overall network. Trust between partners is also essential. Since the boundaries between partners become less rigid, more information flows and there is a risk that this information might be misused. Value networks will therefore not be effective if there is a dominant partner, since trust cannot grow easily in such an environment.

An effective value network can be created if there is a coordinating partner who physically links the value-adding partners and who is independent (not the OEM). For HP's Partner Park, the logistics provider took over this role. This company invested in IT capabilities, offered logistics services for all partners and linked the partners into one common virtual company. If HP had attempted to play this coordinating role, many partners might have felt unwilling to join the network. Other requirements for an effective value network are standardization of IT processes, that services offered between network members should be defined and priced in detail, and that managers should provide an environment that promotes easy and informal communication among employees, since information-sharing is a major asset of this model.

Chapter 7

Fujitsu Siemens Computers: Outsourcing and Supply Chain Mastery

This chapter discusses the combination of initiatives that allow a company in the hypercompetitive PC industry to remain a market leader while producing in Germany. Fujitsu Siemens Computers makes notebooks, PCs, and servers. They have to be disciplined in process improvements and cost reduction, and complement these internal activities with outsourcing to partners to survive in an industry where prices drop so rapidly that 20% volume increases are needed to generate 2% revenue growth. In addition, flexibility and innovation capability are required to tackle newly emerging markets that offer much-needed volume increases.

7.1 Introduction

Fujitsu Siemens Computers (FSC), based in Augsburg in Germany, was founded in 1999 as a 50-50 joint venture between the two major shareholders, Siemens AG (Munich) and Fujitsu Limited (Tokyo). It comprises the former businesses of Fujitsu Computers Europe and Siemens AG's computer systems business in Europe, the Middle East and Africa (EMEA). Its offering extends from notebooks through desktop computers to enterprise-class IT infrastructure solutions and services (Fig. 7.1). Fujitsu Siemens cooperates with Fujitsu in Japan, a broad IT systems and solutions provider. In April 2006, the company added the former Siemens service business unit (with 4,000 employees in 500 service centers across 23 countries) and now offers a wide range of managed, integration, maintenance and financial services. The company has 10,700 employees and operates in all EMEA markets, offering services through its partners in 176 countries.

FSC's manufacturing operations are concentrated in Germany, in Augsburg (the largest site with 1,200 workers, producing professional PCs, mobiles, and servers) and Sömmerda in Thuringia. R&D activities are carried out in Munich, Paderborn, Augsburg, and Sunnyvale (California).

The computer hardware industry, and especially the PC segment, faces cutthroat challenges – extremely fast turnover, price deterioration, and high cost pressure. This is not an environment in which large German companies have done particularly well. Indeed, the merger of Siemens' PC business with Fujitsu's European computer arm was a move that was meant to provide scale and market reach, strengthening the ability of the combined entity to survive.[1] However, the first two years were rough – in 2000–2001, the company shrunk slightly (with €5.9 billion in sales) and made an operating loss. But the company worked hard to become successful: in 2003, the Augsburg site won the IEA award, marking its early achievements in an extremely turbulent and competitive environment.

Fig. 7.1. Fujitsu Siemens Computer notebooks, desktops and servers

The 2003 award was recognition of the Augsburg site's successful mass customization strategy, executed with a focus on supply chain velocity and flexible customization of a modular product for a variety of clients. Manufacturing technology was upgraded every 9 months in order to maintain the company's leading market position and Fujitsu Siemens' flexible assembly lines – which enabled teams to respond to fluctuations in customization demands – were unique in the industry. The customization of each product involved the preloading of software and 5,000 different configurations were installed each month. With its flexible lines, the company achieved end-to-end lead times (from order to delivery) of 8 days.

Warehousing was integrated into the plant, with an external service provider handling materials. With careful forecasting, shared with Asian suppliers, complementing production flexibility, inventory was reduced by 50% to 2–3 weeks' supply. Significantly, its inventory turns were close to Dell's direct distribution

---

[1] The joint venture was assessed in the industry as a response to margin pressures, giving the Siemens computer business the strength to go on, while offering Fujitsu a stronger position in the EMEA markets (see, for example, *ManagerMagazin* 1999; Lambeth 1999).

model. Research and development was shared with Japan; for example, notebooks developed in Japan were sold in EMEA and German-developed servers sold in Japan/Asia.

In order to fulfill the various customer requirements in the different sales channels, FSC developed tailor-made supply chain models. Thirty percent of machines produced were assembled based on predefined product configurations. Fifty percent were assembled with a free-configurable BTO-approach, and the remainder (20%) were assembled with additional customized requirements, such as customer software loads or special services. Fujitsu-Siemens brought its customers into the plant – quite literally. The company hosted the Oktoberfestival, inviting customers, suppliers, and partners to walk the plant over a period of 4 days and see for themselves how the company worked.

Morale was high and pride in the company demonstrated by employees at all levels. One area alone was singled out as a weakness – human resource management, particularly worker participation and knowledge management. Management had already begun to address the perceived weakness in its HR area. Declaring its people the "basis for future success," it was committed to "the development of right skills, competencies and strategic alignment of our people and their devotion, motivation and commitment."

As a result of its strategic positioning and operational improvements, Fujitsu Siemens Computers had conquered the number one position in Germany and number three in Europe in 2003. Unfortunately, this still translated in a slight further revenue contraction, to €5.4 billion; however, the company was earning a positive operating profit and a significant positive cash flow.

7.2 How Do They Do It? By Never Standing Still

After winning the IEA, Fujitsu Siemens accelerated. It achieved steady volume growth, to €6.9 billion in 2007, and was consistently profitable (net profit of €61 million in 2007). A one percent net profit margin looks paltry when seen from many other industries, but in this industry, consistent profitability means success. Augsburg, the main European plant, handles more than five million units a year (out of about 8.5 million units for FSC overall). In 2003, they were turning out 420,000 mobile units; today they are producing more than 1.3 million (three times as many), while the volume for servers doubled, growing from 120,000 to 240,000. And this is in the face of some very hard facts: 20% increase in volume translates into only 2–3% more revenue because unit retail prices are falling all the time. From revenues of €6.9 billion in 2006/2007, the target for 2008 was €7.7 billion and for 2010 €10 billion.[2] Growth on this scale implies a massive increase in volume.

---

[2] Source: Annual Report 2006–2007, interviews.

The question is what does Fujitsu Siemens Computers do in order to remain successful? When we returned to the Augsburg site in 2007, we found a thriving and energetic community that had emphatically not stood still, demonstrating excellence in multiple dimensions.

7.2.1 Strategy

At the top of the company, Bernd Bischoff, President and CEO, maintains that there is no single factor that explains Fujitsu Siemens' success, but that it is a combination of "the right strategy, the right products, the right innovations, the right people, the right partnerships, and the right services." The strategy includes focusing on profitable growth (not growth in its own right) by offering customer-driven solutions in each segment, working with service partners, offering a broad and high-quality service portfolio, emphasizing green (environmentally friendly) products, and all supported by innovation and dedicated employees throughout the company.[3]

At the operational level of the Augsburg site, this general strategy translates into four key execution dimensions: customer orientation of the offering, partnering, iron-fisted process and cost discipline, and employee mobilization. Let's examine how these dimensions are executed.

7.2.2 Customer Orientation

The competitive positioning of the notebooks and servers business in Augsburg is to offer customized data processing solutions that work from day one. Heribert Göggerle, the site manager, describes it as follows: "When you normally get a new PC in the office, it takes you 3 days before it works for you as well as your old one. Ours is fully functional on day one: what normally your company's system administrator, or your value added reseller (VAR) does, we do for the company. We fetch the data from the customers' servers, transfer them to a virtual server on our premises, and then configure the new PCs identically or with the appropriate upgrades. This drives our internal complexity up, because every PC is now different but it creates value for the customers. This cannot be done from China: we have to be close to the customer to do it."

To appreciate the effect of multiple product configurations, consider the following: Augsburg assembles about 50 different product lines (a product refers to a different computer housing). The average life of a product (in production) is 1 year. In other words, one new product ramp-up happens every week on the site.

---

[3] Annual Report 2006–2007.

This position – "We do not just put a box on your desk, we deliver productivity computing power" – enhances customer relationships, and revenue potential, in several ways. First, it directly connects to the service business, in which FSC has greatly enhanced capabilities through the 4,000 new service employees who joined in 2006: the provision of immediately available computing power naturally leads to the exploration of maintenance, support and warranty services (a guaranteed service level for a specified number of years). Plus, the calculation of a product is now no longer based on just hardware, but includes failures, support, and warranties (which used not to be but are now traced back to component suppliers), knowledge that opens up opportunities for cost savings and pricing flexibility. In Göggerle's words, "We are now doing far more than just selling hardware and software."

Second, closer customer interaction allows better feedback on customer needs and problems. This allows Fujitsu Siemens Computers to develop better measures and quality checks based on all field failure data (although the design feedback is only in its infancy and has to be further developed).

Third, in an ongoing relationship that includes a service contract, some of the products' advantages can be much better explained to the customer: a 20% lower energy consumption than competitor products hardly registers with a customer who stares at the one-time purchase price. But once you get monthly service bills, the customer *sees* the lower energy costs, and learns to estimate properly their value the next time round. Thus, the green positioning (which Siemens Nixdorf had begun to develop in the first half of the 1990s) can be translated into real revenues.

The changes described so far apply mainly to the business customer segment. However, FSC is the market leader in Germany for consumer PCs – a crucial segment to capture in order to achieve the volume necessary to benefit from sufficient economies of scale. A major customization drive is under way for this important segment. One new consumer initiative is tackling a major competitor, Dell, head-on. Customers will then be able to order a PC online at a major electronics retail chain and receive it after 24 h. There is direct customer interface: retailers or individual customers can access a Fujitsu Siemens website and configure their computer on a screen. The customized PC is then delivered the next day or day after. There is a restricted choice on this service but it will extend from business to business (B2B) to business to client (B2C), and be the first service of its kind in Germany. Dell and FSC are the only manufacturers worldwide who offer mass customization, configuring systems and machines to order. FSC, however, complements its assemble-to-order production system (which corresponds to Dell's) with a batch system, that is, volumes of pre-defined and pre-assembled base units manufactured in China and shipped to Europe, where they are customized with key components and software. Thus, Fujitsu Siemens Computers can deliver a PC from inventory, or configure to order, enabling a level of flexibility and speed of response that is currently superior to Dell.

7.2.3 Outsourcing and Partnerships

In order to reduce its fixed costs to an affordable level in a low-margin industry, Fujitsu Siemens has relied more and more on other organizations to carry out part of the activities related to its products. This is similar to Hewlett Packard, described in Chap. 6, but Fujitsu Siemens Computers organizes its outsourcing in a different way.

First, FSC relies on an extensive network of 35,000 sales partners worldwide. Some of them are straightforward computer retailers (such as Saturn in Germany and France) who bring the product to the consumer. But in addition many partners collaborate with Fujitsu Siemens to reach industry customers. Local resellers and distributors complement Fujitsu Siemens' own service organization. In addition, Fujitsu Siemens is building a network of solution partners, currently about 2,000 independent software vendors and system integrators who complement the hardware with customized system integration and made-to-order services. All these partners help to expand the market and reach a wider set of customers without the need for Fujitsu Siemens to increase its own organizational infrastructure. Fujitsu Siemens supports these partners with certification, technical services, and sales and marketing intelligence for their customer acquisition efforts.

But working through external organizations does not rest at the sales side. FSC has also outsourced many internal logistics- and production-related activities. For example, production in Augsburg (and increasingly at the second site in Sömmerda) focuses on high-end, technologically intensive motherboards. Low-end boards are manufactured by providers in the Eastern European countries (for example, Romania). New assembly operations in Poland, Russia and Dubai, which address local fast-emerging markets, are executed with certified partners. These partners not only include FSC's investment and risk, but also work in their local network to share capacity, which allows them to respond efficiently to demand fluctuations.

Even activities that stay in Augsburg have been outsourced to external partners. For example, all on-site transport and warehousing activities have been given to a 150-person strong service provider. This provider also works with other companies and can shift personnel between customers (based on a multi-vendor conept), evening out fluctuations in demand from any single customer. This pooling effect makes the provider more efficient than FSC's own internal transport service could be.

Similarly, the distribution center (DC) now operates through a partnership arrangement with an outside supplier. This allowed downsizing from three DCs to one, no bigger than any single DC used previously. Again, this is more efficient because the service provider operates several warehouses, a pooling benefit that allows evening out volume fluctuations at any single site without having to add space.

Over time, Fujitsu Siemens Computers has discovered that an outsourcing initiative is most valuable when it is treated not as a temporary cost reduction arrangement, but as a true partnership: the company works with each service provider for at least 3 years (a long time in the fast moving PC industry), and they look for win-win solutions rather than for one-sided cost squeezing. This embraces two principles: first, open books – everyone knows who makes what saving or profit, which leads to trust and fairness; second, a regular benchmarking process ensures performance pressure based on total performance, not just price.

7.2.4 Iron-Fisted Cost and Process Discipline

A Multitude of Initiatives

With the annual price deterioration that characterizes the computer industry, manufacturers must win additional volume, but they must also become more productive and reduce unit costs. Therefore, FSC has to be obsessed with costs all the time. Maintaining profitability amid falling prices requires a productivity increase of at least 8% per year. "Imagine, our annual costs in logistics and supply chain operations are roughly half a billion Euros," says Göggerle. "We must save between 5% and 8% from that *after* input cost increases, including wage increases."

In order to meet these savings, the company continues its efforts in lean production, driven by process changes as well as employee suggestions (see Sect. 2.5). But in addition, costs have been pared down and systems streamlined in a number of ways. Since 2005, there has been one integrated enterprise resource planning (ERP) system, from the customer all the way to second-tier suppliers, with full flow and cost transparency. Costing project development takes in the whole process, from R&D to manufacturing, and enables early designation of where a product will be developed (either in China or Europe). Forecasting in this way enables tens of millions of Euros savings in shipment costs alone: 80% of material coming from Asia can be transported by boat rather than air.

The product life-cycle of a low-end configuration can be as low as 12 weeks. This poses a problem: the average lead times from China are 12 weeks, so components have to be ordered to fit the entire life cycle volume of each configuration. This places a heavy demand on the efficiency of inventory warehousing and forecasting. In June 2007, spares logistics was integrated in the overall supply chain organization, enabling better purchase negotiations and warehouse productivity – warehousing is shared with original component stock, although at a different service level. Spare part inventories are on track to be reduced by 10–15% through warehouse consolidation.

Technological change is being fast-tracked, because growth will depend on the appearance of new products. Motherboard design is being scaled up, with development based in Germany. For example, a new component placement technology that inserts electronic components on both sides of the motherboard has been introduced – increasing the component density on the board reduces unit costs. The development process is efficient – typically, FSC spends less than €10 million per year on developing desktop PCs, very low for the industry. In addition, the product development managers have been made responsible for a new product throughout its production life-cycle, end-to-end into sales: in other words, their bonuses now partially depend on the sales success of the products they develop. This has given additional urgency to design-to-cost efforts and customer-relevant features, rather than just meeting specifications. A strategic overall view of all initiatives has been initiated in order to maintain consistency and synergies (Fig. 7.2).

The multiple partnering and process improvement efforts have led to a continuing reduction of jobs in production itself, despite the high volume increases. However, only a few of these people have left the company and those who left did so voluntarily; no one has been fired. Most switched to other departments. For example, as Göggerle explains, "I get all field system failures back from the service group and analyze them, which allows me to offer better repair prices. An additional 30 people are employed to do just that, re-internalizing work in the company. The repairers sit in the production area. Additional manpower at this level should soon enable us to incorporate data on systematic failure into product design. This is an ongoing project but many solutions are already available."

In the end, it turns out that all the partnerships and process improvement efforts have not quite been sufficient to avoid touching the core of the wage structure itself. Fujitsu Siemens Computers also decided to increase the normal working week from 35 to 38.5 h (and in some administrative jobs from 40 to 44 h) to spread the fixed costs of labor over more units. Although the taboo of extending the 35-h working week was broken by several companies in Germany in 2005–2006, this was very painful. However, the labor cost comparison was too striking: a comparable production job costs $90 per month in China, versus $3,100 in Germany. Until 2006, the speed and flexibility advantages had been enough to counteract the cost disadvantage: 85% of Augsburg's production that was custom assembled could be produced and shipped within 1 day, as against 10 days if

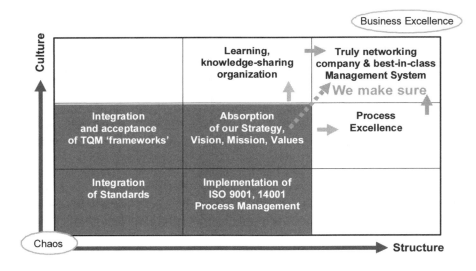

Fig. 7.2. Business excellence strategy of FSC's operational improvements

shipped from China. In addition, flexible working times could help to handle strong demand variation from day to day.[4]

But when the computer market contracted in mid 2006, management questioned the viability of the German production sites (Fujitsu Siemens is the only large computer maker still producing in Germany) and started pushing for an extension of the working week to 40 h. Negotiations with unions and worker councils lasted 9 months before an agreement was reached in February 2007 to extend the week to 38.5 h without wage increase. Employees could choose to work more hours or stay at 35 h, but this would entail a wage reduction. In turn, Fujitsu Siemens Computers guaranteed maintaining 4,750 jobs in Germany until 2010 and ruled out business-related layoffs.

This was, of course, a controversial and potentially demotivating turn of events. However, the emphasis was on saving jobs in Germany under adverse conditions.[5] Unions and worker councils grudgingly agreed to the arrangement. Employees accepted that in a situation where no other computer company had retained any manufacturing in Germany, the change was justifiable. Still, this negative event made efforts in employee participation and motivation even more important – and this is what we turn to now.

7.2.5 Employee Mobilization

In spite of the negative work week changes, Fujitsu Siemens Computers has made a major effort to inform, involve, and mobilize all employees. In different parts of the company, this effort had different names, such as the "we make sure" initiative and the "innovation starts on the CEO's desk" initiative.

The "innovation starts on the CEO's desk" innovation initiative was begun in all German sites in 2005, with an innovation tool – described simply as "the best" – devised in partnership with the Fraunhofer Institute for Applied Information Technology in Bonn. The tool allows anyone at all in the company to enter ideas and management response is guaranteed within 8 or 9 days. Use of the tool is disseminated through on-site innovation days, when two innovation ideas each are demonstrated in workshops of 15 employees. An annual award is offered for the best idea presented. The innovation initiative received the Boston Consulting Group innovation prize in 2007.

In parallel to the innovation initiative, FSC ran its "we make sure" brand initiative, designed to make sure that everyone in the company understood the strategy, to involve all employees, and to reinforce their mental model about reliability and responsibility. The initiative emphasized that business excellence involves not only process improvement but also change in behavior, by both management and operators.

---

[4] Ehrensberger 2006.
[5] DPA ticker, February 8, 2007.

There were workshops involving all 2,000 employees on site, symbolizing their own company with a restaurant: "Which restaurant would you go back to? The one with the lowest price, the one with the best food, or reliable speed, or nice service?" Then, "Explain what each employee contributes to the success criteria – the chef, the waiter, the cleaner, the security guard? Who contributes what in the service chain?" And then, returning to Fujitsu Siemens, "What do *you* contribute?" Göggerle describes the workshops as follows:

> People develop this knowledge experientially. As a result, for example, production people entered in discussion with purchasing people and challenged them: this marked the start of a change in mindset. People wrote down what they would improve, and some submitted their ideas. Seven hundred suggestions about strategy cascading and leadership behavior were contributed in Augsburg alone, and included queries such as: how often is an area manager (VP) on the shop floor? How often does he give feedback? This was a true bottom-up process, and it took three months.

The workshops were followed up by an annual employee survey. Still, without regular active events, and in the context of the controversial work week negotiations, the "energy" around involvement decreased once more. In the summer of 2007, the workshops were revived, this time including some key suppliers and partners with their personnel in the process. Management has found that maintaining employee positive attitude and involvement is an ongoing process: if people are not reminded and energized, it tends to wane.

The innovation and "we make sure" initiatives are complemented by formal performance and career management systems and processes. For example, managers have a performance-variable pay component of up to 40%, and even front line salaried employees have a variable pay component of 15%. In addition, about 40 (of 1,200) salaried employees in Augsburg (excluding operators) are classified as either local or global talent based on performance criteria. "Global talents" are given global opportunities (in a formalized cross-country process) and may be moved at relatively short notice.

7.3 Still Getting Better?

If this chapter so far has given the impression that Fujitsu Siemens Computers is working hard to optimize a stable system, that impression is wrong: all improvements have to be chased while the environment is far from stable. Not only is a new generation of each computer model coming out on average once per year, but the segments and markets themselves are changing. As we explained earlier, achieving growth is critical for survival in an industry with strong price erosion; the key for success lies in Fujitsu Siemens' ability to pursue changing markets.

7.3.1 New Segments and Markets

The market is shifting from desktops to notebooks and, more generally, mobile products. But new market segments are also arising. For example, more and more older people are buying PCs, customers who are less computer and technology savvy than the young. There seems to be an opportunity in offering these people an "all taken care of" product, with remote diagnostics, for a monthly fee paid by subscription. Fujitsu Siemens' services business unit makes the company well placed to develop this market segment.

FSC is also committed to extending its leadership in environmentally friendly products, an initiative it began in 2002 with the production of the first non-lead PCBs. In 2005–2006, Greenpeace gave Fujitsu Siemens five out of seven possible points in its annual environmental product evaluation, making the company the green leader in the field of PC manufacturing. As in the automotive industry, the environmentally conscious market segment is likely to grow, providing opportunities to be followed up.

In addition to market segments, market regions are also changing. Within FSC's main market of EMEA, the relative weight is rapidly shifting toward Eastern Europe and the Arab world, with Poland and Russia proving the fastest growing. Fujitsu Siemens is moving to be able to serve these markets, working with partners, as we described in Sect. 2.3.

The next step is to take servers into Asia and the US. This part of the business is still small but growing rapidly. In Fujitsu Siemens' joint venture agreement, the US is classified as a Fujitsu market, but Fujitsu has focused on high-end products and is dissatisfied with growth, so they allow FSC to take the low- to mid-range products there – "made in China, engineered by Fujitsu Siemens Computers in Europe" – on the basis of the company's proven European success. FSC is now delivering its notebooks from China directly to the United States.

7.3.2 Keep Running to Succeed

In the fast moving and hypercompetitive computer industry, you have to run hard just to stand still. The outlook is uncertain for all players in the industry. By 2007, even mighty Dell had begun to sell its European consumer products through an indirect channel, Carrefour, in effect modifying its business model. FSC was ahead of this competitor, in building a double-channel structure, by several years.

In this environment, it will take continuing efforts and ingenuity for Fujitsu Siemens Computers and its Augsburg site to continue to succeed. Indeed, the company has lost revenues and even some market share in professional PCs and enterprise products (while gaining in services), and critics point to the low profit margins and speculate whether the joint venture agreement between Fujitsu and

Siemens will be renewed when it comes up for review in 2009.[6] Of course, the need to satisfy shareholders is nothing new – if the company continues to use its capabilities to improve and to adapt to new markets, it will be able to create value and maintain the support of its shareholders.

---

[6] Hofer 2007.

Chapter 8

RDME: Re-Importing Jobs from Brazil

This chapter shows a wonderful example of how a large international company, CVRD, turned around a dispirited and financially challenged metal works, using an excellent management team that applied management quality and continuous improvement. The resources of the international company, in terms of investment as well as knowledge and leadership, saved RDME. The interesting twist in this story is that the failing organization, RDME, was in France, and the mother company, CVRD, in Brazil: Europeans and Americans have to say good-bye to the comfortable old notion that they know best and export their superior knowledge to the rest of the world. The ultimate benefit from foreign investments and trade is that knowledge starts coming back and is exchanged, a dynamic that has the potential to make everyone better off in the end.

8.1 History of a Turnaround

The Brazilian firm CVRD (Compania Vale do Rio Doce) is the world's largest iron ore company. CVRD purchased 100% of a troubled ferromanganese plant located in Grande-Synthe, near Dunkerque, France, to establish RDME (Rio Doce Manganese Europe) in 2000. The plant, which contains the largest ferromanganese furnace in the world, was built by the French firm Usinor in the early 1990s in an attempt to break a cartel in Europe. CVRD purchased 35% of the facility in 1992 and contributed technical expertise that allowed for the processing of non conventional minerals, such as those from CVRD's Carajàs mine in Brazil. While initial results in the first half of the 1990s exceeded many expectations, price competition initiated by Usinor in the face of their competitor Eramet had taken a significant toll on the operation. In 1999, it lost money, the facility was degraded, jobs were lost, and morale was low.

CVRD also had several mines and plants in Brazil, and represents a well-known name in metallurgy. However, its manganese division was troubled, and lost US$44 million in 1998. With a lack of potential acquirers, CVRD rethought its strategy for the future. The opportunity to control significant capacity in Europe with the complete purchase of Usinor's plant in Dunkerque represented an excellent opportunity to gain a foothold in Europe and increase market share in the region.

8.1.1 The Product and the Process

Manganese (Mn) is critical for steel production, and is used in cars, large household appliances and many other daily goods. Manganese is a grayish metal with properties similar to iron, occurs in a number of minerals, and is exploitable through rocks and fines. Approximately 90% of the world's demand for manganese ore is ultimately used by the steel industry. Of that, approximately 84% is used in alloys. Fines must be processed by sinterization before being processed in a furnace.

In a sinter plant, manganese ore is combined with coke; the material is then heated, and becomes fused into sinter, an agglomeration about 10–15 cm in diameter. If the fines were not sintered, they would tend to clog the furnace before dropping into the furnace and melting. The sinter can then be sold on the spot market to steel producers, or input to the furnace for alloy production. The furnace at Grande-Synthe produces 120–140 k tons per year of ferromanganese alloys, including FeSiMn (a low grade alloy), FeMnHC (high carbon alloy), and FeMnMC/LC (medium or low carbon). Four times per day, 100 tons of liquid ferromanganese alloys pour from the base of the furnace. After cooling, the ferromanganese is fractured into pieces before shipping via truck or train to clients. In addition to alloys, rich slag is skimmed off the flow from the furnace. In addition to FeMn alloys and slag, the furnace also releases gases, which are cleaned and burned. The average holding time of materials in RDME's furnace is 16 h.

8.1.2 Early Changes

On arrival at the plant in June 1999, the new CEO of RDME, Luis Carlos Nepomuceno, developed his team locally and was joined by Charles Rezende, who landed in France from Brazil a year later to serve as Finance and Administrative Director, followed by Brazilian Marciano Batista as Industrial Director, as well several other team members. The team was faced with monumental challenges. Although the plant was well located with respect to the port of Dunkerque, railroads, canal and highway networks, they found a rundown plant, a demotivated workforce, and financial troubles. At the same time, the South Americans were intensively learning the French language. The plant had received ISO 9002 certification in 1996 prior to CVRD acquiring the plant, but processes in general were not operated in a standardized manner, and there were a number of environmental concerns to address. These issues were tackled immediately with measures aligned with the firm's priorities for improved communication between management and the workforce: technological investment; training of personnel and incentives for continuous improvement; action for cleanliness, the environment, and safety; and process standardization.

During a site visit by the IEA team in February 2002, we observed the results of those ongoing initiatives. Processes had been brought under control and were stable. In addition, a change in working atmosphere and culture had been initiated and was on its way of changing the way the plant operated. The main themes were:

- Social development: communication, training
- Environmental and safety improvement
- Client satisfaction
- Industrial, finance and economic performance

The new style of communication was characterized by Nepomuceno as requiring "big ears and a small mouth." By 2001, office space was significantly reorganized, so that many walls were removed (Fig. 8.1). The few offices with walls maintained an "open door" policy, which was perceived to be a key to resolving problems before they became crises. Employee satisfaction was high, and communication between the operational staff, administrative staff, and management had become comfortable. Internal newsletters and magazines were established.

Other dimensions of social development involved training. Employees were offered technical training, and language courses in Portuguese, English, or French. Exchange programs were set up for visits between CVRD in Brazil and RDME in France lasting a week, 3 months or a year. A results sharing scheme reinforced the motivation in the workforce. Worker training represented 5.4% of salary costs, and the annual turnover rate of employees was 1%.

Quality function deployment (QFD) and the 5S concepts were deployed in a form customized to local conditions (the "*cinq actes*" in RDME's terminology). Most significantly, the 5S concepts were not only applied to workstations but to the entire facility. Environmental efforts included cleaning up messy fines, and the refurbishment of the exterior and interior of buildings. Marciano Batista explained how the short paved road leading from the main offices to the furnace and sinterization plant "used to be a dusty or muddy field worn from heavy vehicles" that was

Fig. 8.1. Transformation of administrative space from closed (*left*) to open (*right*) space through 2001

not clean for plant visits, but "now allows for clean, safe access to the facilities" (see Fig. 8.2). The programs relied significantly on employee participation at all levels. Ideas from suggestion boxes chosen for implementation were moved forward with significant direction from the proposer, usually the person responsible for the process. Managers would give a direct explanation why an idea from the suggestion boxes was not to be pursued to the employee who suggested it.

Industrial process improvements with the deployment of new technologies were apparent in several areas. SAP R3 software was purchased to help standardize procurement. Process control software was implemented to improve control for sinterization. The furnace is highly reliable, and is controlled with state-of-the-art software (Fig. 8.3) that allows the "pilots" to take control if needed.

Fig. 8.2. Access to the site before (*left*) and after (*right*) the clean-up process

Fig. 8.3. Control room for ferromanganese furnace at RDME

The sinterization process almost doubled in productivity because of a combination of continuous improvement measures and commercial development in new markets to utilize that capacity. Benchmarking and certification also played a role, and were facilitated by the exchange programs with Brazil and internal steps to document processes. ISO 9002 certification was already in place in 1995. The 5S programs helped lead to ISO 14001 environmental certification in September 2001, a first for a ferro alloy furnace, followed by the UIC environmental prize in November 2001. The UIC is a professional organization for the chemical industry in France that rewards continuous improvement in environmental issues that goes beyond legal obligations.

Competition in 2001 was based on a motivated team, the CVRD brand name, the ability to draw upon the natural resources in CVRD's mines in Brazil, the integration of high-quality CVRD mineral resources with RDME production, a high productivity furnace, and logistics. Customer satisfaction initiatives included the transhipment of other metals from CVRD Brazil to clients in Europe, initiatives to work toward ISO 9002 recertification, and reliable shipment. New markets for delivery to Spain, Italy, Norway, and Eastern Europe were explored. The plant is well situated for easy reception of minerals sent by sea, for rail and roadway distribution to clients, and access to some major clients, including a Usinor plant about a kilometer away. The open management style not only enabled the motivation of the team, but also extended to good relationships with suppliers and governmental bodies.

Environmental and safety improvement initiatives assumed several forms, such as changes to the physical infrastructure, recycling and worker safety programs, and ISO 14001 certification. The transformation of the site also had symbolic elements that demonstrated the general upgrade: for example, the old office building was transformed into the Sustainable Development Exhibition – CVRD (L'Espace Rio Doce). The exhibition traces the history and operation of CVRD. The space also illustrates the history, people, culture, and environment of Brazil with films, pictures of both urban and Amazon jungle settings, scale models of mines, and samples of rainforest seeds. The resource serves as a site for special events like retirement ceremonies, meetings, and outings for schools. "We wanted a facility that focused on sharing culture, openness, one that explained not only the plant and the supply chain from Brazil, but also to celebrate people and their environments," explains Luis Carlos Nepomuceno.

The transformation led to impressive financial results. In 1999, the gross margin was a loss of almost €1.1 million on €58.7 million in sales. By 2001, gross margins were €9.3 million on €102.6 million in sales. Employment grew from 98 permanent and temporary employees in 1999 to 116 employees in 2001. Annual production of sinter grew from 229 thousand tons to 392 thousand tons, resulting in a significant decrease in previously unusable inventories of fines at CVRD Brazil. Annual production of FeMn alloys increased from 120 thousand to 132 thousand tons through that period. The progress gained the plant an IEA prize in 2002, with special mention for human resources and knowledge management.

8.2 Development After 2002: Growing and Creating Jobs

From 2002 the management team continued relentless improvements along several fronts: internally, investments in further automation and technical improvements were combined with further changes in personnel policies. Externally, RDME won additional customers (most notably the British steel company Corus) and tackled two major business expansions, the first the acquisition of an additional furnace in Mo i Rana, Norway, the second the addition of a new product, cored wire, in Grande-Synthe.

8.2.1 Operational Improvements

RDME continued to invest in technical improvements, at a pace of €2–4 million per year. For example, the control system (hardware and software) was repeatedly upgraded, to make the furnace the most automated of its kind in the world today. Two operators per 8-h shift are sufficient to monitor and control operations 24 h per day. After 13 years of operation, the furnace was revamped and relined from April 7 to June 19, 2004. The cooling system was upgraded, and an improved off-gas washing system installed, which reduced emissions and improved efficiency simultaneously. This caused a drop in productivity in 2004 relative to 2003, but productivity after the relining increased 5–8%.

The improvements included investments in safety; for example, several certifications were achieved (ISO 9001 version 2000, OHSAS 18001), which included a number of procedural changes. As a result, the plant has worked over 2,000 days without a single accident. During the furnace relining, 140 people from 40 companies worked for 75,000 h without a serious accident.

Engineering improvements went in parallel with ongoing continuous improvement efforts. Improvement projects ebb and flow, but in the long-run average, the engineering manager estimates that every employee spends about 30 min per day, representing about 6% of work time, on improvement activities that are non-productive in the very short term. Although the big improvements stem from engineering-driven changes, continuous improvement efforts by all employees do contribute significantly – perhaps around 30% – to overall productivity progress. This is remarkable: in a highly automated facility, the small improvement ideas contributed by shop floor workers add half as much again to productivity improvements as the large-scale engineering driven improvements. This is an illustration of the power of worker mobilization in the context of well-mastered processes.

The ongoing continuous improvement is supported by a suggestion scheme with rewards, by a heavy emphasis on training (9 days per employee per year in Grande-Synthe, corresponding to 8% of total salary costs, which is high in comparison to other companies across industries), and by continued investment in cleanliness (5S) around the furnace, the sinter plant, and the entire site (Figs. 8.1 and 8.2). Training includes on-the-job training, job rotation, visits to Brazil for managers and high-level technicians, as well as specialized technical training courses. As François Lavallée, the HR director, comments, "We were 'franco-français,' but now we have a more international outlook. For example, 25% of our people have taken a course in English or Portuguese."

Finally, RDME has also leveraged other activities of the mother company CVRD in Europe: CVRD delivers two million tons of iron ore to European steel makers. RDME used those established shipping connections to piggy-back the much smaller manganese ore transports (150,000 tons) on other transports, saving costs.

8.2.2 Personnel Policies

In people management, Luis Carlos Nepomuceno and his team pushed further improvements relentlessly. The open door policy was extended and made extremely visible: in the new administration building, offices have been completely abandoned, so that even the walls depicted in the "open" areas in the right half of Fig. 8.1 were removed. Everyone sits in an open space, not even separated by cubicle walls, including top management. Everyone can see everyone else all the time. "This was difficult, as it does not correspond to traditional French management culture. But people have accepted it, and now it feels very good because we can very easily communicate with one another," recounts Nepomuceno.

The emphasis on team work, and the recognition of the contribution of all employees, is pervasive and consistent; it has become part of the company culture. It starts at the top when Nepomuceno states that "good motivated people are the way to success," and lives the motto in his behavior, and it continues when the engineering manager, Marcelo Rocha, goes to talk to the control operators at the furnace. The atmosphere is one of pride, where everyone is willing to take an extra step on their own initiative.

Motivation and initiative do not come at the expense of safety or productivity – for example, Marcelo Rocha has access to the real-time furnace control system from home and can see at any point in time what is going on.

The company culture continues to evolve. New official reward schemes are being introduced in parallel with profit-sharing ("*intéressement*") based on company results, group-based, and individual bonuses. In addition, every employee is assigned a "godfather," a more senior mentor who helps him or her in career planning, as part of a program initiated in 2002. Everyone has a yearly performance review and goal setting conversation with his or her superior. And employees have the opportunity to progress in their career if they want to – for example, the CFO started as a purchasing clerk. Human resources has a database with career status, development needs, and succession planning for every employee.

In this atmosphere, the collaboration with the unions (CGT and CFDT) has become more constructive (although collaboration between unions and management is never easy). Marcelo Rocha comments, "Before I came here, I did not believe that it was possible to be open and listen to the workers, undertake measures to the environment, *and* be highly productive, all at the same time. The key is motivated people – it *is* possible to constructively work with people here. At home, people do not have the mindset to change. This is one of the main lessons I will take home with me."

The good working atmosphere was rewarded with external recognition in December 2004. RDME was awarded 11th ranking in the French journal *Management*'s competition for the "Best Places to Work" in France, ahead of companies like Deloitte, Novartis, Computer Associates, Auchan and Bosch. This is a spectacular success for a small subsidiary of a Latin American company in an industry that is perceived as dirty and the opposite of sexy. It attests how far the company has come in motivating employees with an attractive work environment.

8.2.3 External and Customer Relationships

Manganese and ferromanganese alloys are commodity products – in principle there is nothing in the chemical composition that distinguishes one producer from the other. However, RDME has successfully managed to acquire a reputation for reliability – they deliver consistent product quality, quickly and on time.

Quick delivery is related to RDME's location in the center of industrial Europe, right next door to a huge Arcelor steel plant and close to Germany and the UK. However, RDME has also worked hard to move from arm's-length, spot market type of interactions with customers to longer-term relationships. This happens through the central CVRD sales office in Europe, but also directly through ongoing operational relationships between RDME and the customer. Longer-term relationships offer a win-win situation for both sides, helping RDME to understand what the customers need and flexibly adapting the product mix and shipping conditions, and protecting the customers from short-term price swings.

Part of the offering is a logistics service that allowed RDME to deliver product just-in-time to the customer's steel plant. No competitor can offer this type of service. Dunkerque benefits from an excellent location along the coast, with access to every possible means of transport (i.e., vessel, barge, truck, train). The harbor equipment is cheap and efficient and accepts even large capesize vessels. The shipping department and transportation follow-up department has three people in Dunkerque, and another in Brussels who is responsible for maritime logistics and sales planning. As a result, RDME won the large UK steel company Corus as a customer, and also expanded its customer base into Spain, Italy, and Eastern Europe.

RDME has also improved relationships with its suppliers, again looking for win-win opportunities for closer collaboration. Annual reviews with all strategic suppliers examine quality, lead time and reactivity for delivery, price, respect for the environment, and compliance with safety procedures. Suppliers are contacted find ways to cooperate and improve the performance of their products and services. One recent example is collaboration with Van Miegen Leclerc, contracted for work in the tapping area. Others include collaboration with Elkem to adapt the quality of carbon pastes in order to decrease electrode breakage, and collaboration with FAI, to reduce electrical power consumption. This does not sound revolutionary judged by the standards of the automotive industry, but it is quite unusual in ore processing.

Finally, RDME views and manages relationships with the local community in the same way. The company actively contributes to community life and support projects in Grande-Synthe. In December 2003, RDME received the Grande-Synthe Prize as one of the most dynamic and innovative companies in the district, honoring their new activities, job creation and community support in the town. Good community relationships are rewarding in themselves and motivating, but they may also improve business: after restarting the furnace RDME encountered some problems with increased smoke discharging into the atmosphere. But, thanks to permanent and transparent management of the environmental issues, and some continuous and voluntary relationships with the local authorities, RDME was given additional notice to enable them to explain better the measures taken to ameliorate the discharge.

8.2.4 Expansion of Activities

With the strengths it has put in place over the last 5 years, RDME (and CVRD's manganese division in general) has set itself the goal of moving from the number three producer worldwide (behind Eramet and BHP Billiton) to the number one position by 2010. Since 2002, RDME has been looking at expansion opportunities. Two have already been executed.

The first is the acquisition of a furnace from Elkem in the small town of Mo i Rana in northern Norway, on the Arctic Circle (Fig. 8.4). RDME scanned competitors in search of a facility they could buy without increasing industry capacity overall (thus avoiding general price pressure). They also explored building a second furnace in Grande-Synthe, but the project was temporarily shelved when EDF did not offer an attractive energy contract. Then they came across a bankrupt chrome smelter in Mo i Rana, which was about to be closed down: only a core team of 20 was still there, the other 60 had been let go, and the end for those 20 was also in sight.

The plant had a special energy contract with the Norwegian energy provider at $7 per KWh, with a market price of $22. The energy could thus be re-sold in the external market at a profit, which had accumulated to €17 million. The catch was that the energy contract did not allow expatriation of the profit out of the community, so it just sat there. Eramet had been offered the company before but had declined. RDME analyzed the situation and then grabbed it.

Fig. 8.4. RDMN facility in Mo i Rana, Norway

They paid €17 million as the acquisition price, and then used the internally accumulated energy trading profits and US$10 million to convert the chrome smelter for ferromanganese alloys, completely revamping it in the process. On June 30, 2003, the first furnace started up, and the second followed in November. During the year 2003, RDMN (Rio Doce Manganese Norway) made a profit of €8 million through trading the cheap energy, under the initiative of Marciano Batista who moved from Dunkerque to Norway. By 2004, RDMN had 72 full time employees and produced a real operating profit. Trond Saeterstad was sent to Brazil for training and assumed the position of managing director in January 2005, replacing the last Brazilian at RDMN. He reports to Luis Carlos Nepomuceno, as the head of CVRD Manganese International.

RDMN applied the same personnel polices as RDME, and the effects on positive employee morale and initiative rapidly became visible.

This example demonstrates RDME's strength in having a clear strategy that allows them to recognize opportunities, and to seize them quickly with opportunistic flexibility. The cheap energy contract allowed RDME to acquire the company under attractive conditions, but this was not the deal rationale, it merely reinforced a clear strategy: it would enable RDME's expansion in Europe, while allowing them to enter the US market. Manganese imports from Brazil into the US were banned because of anti-dumping legislation in the US. But RDMN did not fall under this law, so it opened a huge additional potential market for CVRD.

RDME had foreseen price deterioration of 5% because of the capacity that they were adding to the industry with the Norwegian furnaces. However, luck was also on their side over this, as steel and steel ingredient prices strongly rose in 2003 and even further during 2004. Another risk was the termination of the cheap energy contract in 2005; currently, there are renegotiations under way, which RDMN undertakes together with 100 other companies in the Mo i Rana business park. Many of the other companies in the business park are weaker than RDMN and would be seriously endangered by market energy prices.

The second business expansion went on line in 2004. RDME constructed a calcium–silicon (CaSi) cored wire facility. Cored wire is hollow wire produced from a steel band that is mechanically coiled (bent) around crystallized powder such as manganese silicon (MnSi) and other compositions. Manganese silicon is an ingredient in steel making that allows fine-tuning of the characteristics of the steel (such as strength, corrosion resistance, brittleness). The cored wire allows the steel maker to dose the chemical very precisely by ensuring that all the material is introduced deep into the smelter and does not evaporate at the surface.

Again, this project combined a clear strategic rationale with opportunistically flexible execution. This facility rounded out the bundle of services and flexible offerings that strengthened RDME's long-term value proposition to its customers. In executing it, RDME paid none of the €2 million start-up costs itself: it received 20% as a subsidy from the region, and financed 80% through loans. The business was auto-financing. In turn, RDME hired 25, mostly young, people to run the facility.

The plant is highly automated, reflecting low margins for this type of product. A dispenser pours manganese silicon powder into the half-bent wire that runs through the bending machine. The wire is then fully bent around and closed and then automatically coiled. The plant is operated by three shifts of five people; all administration is handled by two staff and one general manager.

8.3 Lessons

RDME's clear strategy of growth in Europe, part of the internationalization strategy of CVRD, has taken advantage of market opportunities. They gained competitive advantage through consistent product quality, reliability of deliveries, and productivity. Location plays a key role in Dunkerque, both because of port access for the delivery of raw materials, and also for distribution to customers, several of whom are close by (Arcelor, Corus, and Krupp Thyssen).

The strategy combines an overall vision with flexible execution that exploits opportunities as they arise. Examples include innovation in the sinterization process to convert unused stockpiles of fines into usable raw materials for sinter and alloys. The expansion into Mo i Rana brought with it an excellent energy contract and locally usable cash. Although this added 110,000 tons per year capacity to the ferro alloys market and raised the possibility of price decreases, the increased capacity allowed for further energy efficiency renovation of the Dunkerque furnace, and prices were unaffected due to an increase in demand. Mo i Rana also allowed entry into the US market via Norway, circumventing an embargo on Latin American imports. Finally, the expansion into cored wire was achieved with a subsidy and bank loans, to enable a self-financing operation that provides an additional service to their clients.

The operations strategy for achieving these gains puts people at the center. Luis Carlos Nepomuceno explains, "Good people lead to a better bottom line. Openness and training lead to motivation which leads to continuous improvement. Improvement leads to a better bottom line, growth, and job satisfaction. High-quality automation adds to productivity improvement." Nepomuceno and the management team consistently sought win-win situations in relationships with all stakeholders: customers, employees, unions, suppliers, and the community. The result is a more educated workforce, more jobs, student access to the Sustainable Development Center, and a constructive relationship with officialdom about environmental impact, not to mention higher production capacity and revenues.

For a plant in a basic materials industry that is flat overall, the results are impressive. Employment doubled from 97 to 195 in Europe (including Norway), and revenues have almost tripled in 6 years, through competitiveness and the pursuit of new markets.

Productivity enhancements are needed if RDME is to stay competitive. Conquering new markets allows for growth in employment that would not otherwise happen in the presence of productivity enhancements. Capacity growth, such as RMME/RDMN achieved in Norway, alleviates the bottleneck that arises from productivity enhancements and market growth. These three factors are linked in producing growth in industrialized countries.

PART IV

What Does This Mean? Implications of the Industrial Excellence Examples

Chapter 9

Offshoring and Jobs: Zyme, Dyson, and Some General Lessons

In this chapter, we discuss two examples of companies who practice off-shoring, shifting activities into so-called developing (or low-wage) countries. This is widely criticized for allegedly being done for reasons of cost reduction alone, and off-shoring companies are frequently accused of destroying jobs at home. However, the examples in this chapter demonstrate that proactive strategic off-shoring is not simply done for reasons of cost and can create both value and jobs at home. The lesson for companies is not to use outsourcing in a purely defensive manner, focusing on cost-cutting for existing activities. That is a losing proposition in the long run. Outsourcing can be used proactively to widen the range of things that a company can do, and increase competitiveness. At the end of this chapter, we provide evidence that off-shoring can indeed lead to job creation (although to be sure, some low-skilled jobs will inevitably be lost to Eastern Europe and the Far East). First we review the examples of Zyme and Dyson, in the USA and the UK, before returning to the central themes of the off-shoring debate and the perceived contradiction between company competitiveness and job creation in the surrounding economy.

9.1 Zyme Solutions

Zyme Solutions was founded in 2004 by Chandran Sankaran, an experienced manager with previous responsibilities as a consultant, then Vice President at a leading supply chain management software company, and then founder of a successful start-up that he had sold a year earlier. Zyme offered outsourced analytic services to cleanse, validate, mine and model channel data for high technology customers with dispersed sales channels, and transform them into meaningful information. Its headquarters was in Redwood City, California, close to the heart of Silicon Valley.[1]

9.1.1 The Customer Problem

Zyme's typical customer profile was a medium to large high-tech company that sold its products through a network of hundreds of partners, distributors, and resellers around the world, ranging from large distributors to mom-and-pop stores in

---

[1] The description of Zyme Solutions Inc. is taken from Loch and Wu 2006.

Taiwan and Eastern Europe. The customer needed to know inventory levels and point-of-sale (POS) sell-through, in order to manage inventory, adjust production volume and mix, compensate the channel, and run marketing actions.

Customers recognized channel tracking as important (indeed, mission critical), but at the same time it was not considered to be a core competence. It was certainly not a line of work that was perceived as "leading somewhere." Tracking channel information was a nightmare. Usually, channel partners sent POS and inventory data once a week but the data were presented in a wide variety of formats, including Excel spreadsheets, faxes, text files, and so on. Moreover, the data were plagued by inaccuracies, like incorrect dates, invalid stock keeping unit (SKU) numbers, typographical errors, and missing records.

A company with 300 resellers would have between five and ten people spread over the US, Europe, and Asia, consolidating data in one central data warehouse. Taken on as analysts who would be instrumental in making policy suggestions, these employees ended up inputting, cleaning and consolidating data from different regions. Discrepancies at quarter end were sometimes in the order of millions of dollars and analyst groups were often demotivated and suffered from high turnover.

Some customers simply had no effective data management. Others coped but felt the work could be done much better and more efficiently, while yet others wanted to introduce incentive programs for their channel partners that required tracking volumes and prices and calculating rebates based on complex incentive formulas, and found that they did not have the capability to do so.

These were the reasons why these companies were looking for service partners. However, outsourcing a mission-critical function was sensitive: the clients were only willing to outsource channel tracking after thorough due diligence and trust building. Several of the early customers were willing to talk to a young and small company like Zyme only because they had known Chandran Sankaran through interactions in his previous positions and his first company.

But once a customer had come to know Zyme, they saw a real difference. One customer commented:

> It became clear that Zyme's competitor relied on the same technologies that we would have had to rely on, so they faced the same reliability issues. Zyme had smart people to back up their proposal, with the ability to react flexibly to challenges with the data. They really understood our business needs, and they offered us a risk-minimizing deal with monthly payments and the option for us to take the job back.

Zyme was also one of the cheapest bidders, but that was not seen as decisive. "The other company had a good sales pitch, but Zyme came across as sincere and flexible, and they had a very trustworthy reference. And they have not let us down a single time." Zyme quickly established a good reputation, and early customers served as references for the next wave of customers.

9.1.2 The Front End

Zyme had different ways of collecting the data for different clients. Ideally, all files from the channel partners arrived at the customer's central server and were auto-forwarded from there directly to a client-specific production queue in Zyme's Indian operations center, without any client action at all. This forwarding process could be implemented within a week (some clients still preferred to forward the files manually).

Once the forwarding process was set up, the files with weekly channel information entered Zyme's production system from Saturday to Monday. The operations team in Bangalore processed, cleaned, and consolidated the files as they came in. Once a day, Zyme uploaded cleaned high-quality data (data with a high degree of accuracy and consistency) back to the client's data warehouse (see Fig. 9.1). If a file failed to arrive, or was below standard (with discrepancies, for example) Zyme got in touch with their contact at the customer base, who called the channel partner to obtain the correct file. Several customers decided to delegate this first-level corrective action to Zyme as well – in these cases, Zyme called the channel partner directly.

By Wednesday, Zyme had usually uploaded 99% of the files, and started on the analysis. This included a summary report across all files, and a partner score-card indicating which partner had sent the data, whether they were on time, etc. In addition, Zyme sent back an exception report including, for example, trend changes, or inconsistencies (typically 10–15 exceptions per week and per client).

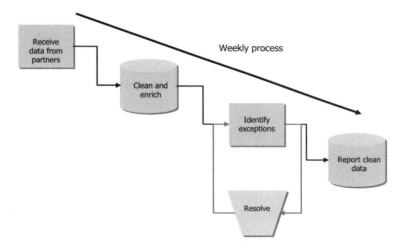

Fig. 9.1. Weekly data cleaning process

Figure 9.2 is an example of Zyme's data reconciliation. The table shows the inventory reported in the previous week, the inventory the client shipped into the channel, the reported inventory of the current week, and finally, the discrepancies between the calculated inventory and the reported inventory. This detailed reconciliation allowed the identification of anomalies and trends that were flagged to the client.

The analysts in the Indian operations center not only performed routine analyses, but took the initiative to go beyond mere data processing. For example, the exception reports were offered from within the operations center. Similarly, the center proposed revenue performance reports per channel partner and per region in a graphical format, price exception analyses, and roll-forward reconciliation (inventory + shipments − sales = inventory next period) that allowed much tighter plausibility checking of the numbers. Not all clients were using all the available reports, but once Zyme proposed them, clients generally appreciate them. Some clients even began to use Zyme to administer special promotion offers (track the sales after the promotion and calculate the special incentives per distributor depending on their performance). Zyme was consistently a step ahead of their clients in proposing useful extensions of the service that the client had not considered but found invaluable once they used them.

The "face" of Zyme was the Client Service Manager (CSM), who linked the clients in the US with the operations team in India. The CSM understood both the operations processes in India and the business processes in the customer's organization, including sales, production planning, and commission criteria for the channel partners. In 2006, Zyme had five CSMs, and on average each was responsible for three customers.

The CSM had weekly, occasionally daily, communications with a counterpart in the customer's organization (usually a project manager in sales operations or finance) who understood the data collection process and was involved in channel management. In addition, the CSM had a weekly operations meeting over the telephone with the customer, going through the exception report, and discussing operations issues, such as missing files and misreported inventories. The CSM

Part Number	Month	Aug-05				Aug-05
	Fiscal Week End Date	8/6/2005	8/13/2005	8/20/2005	8/26/2005	
967415-0403	Beginning Inv (Calculated)	4,246	3,811	689	742	4,246
	Minus POS	(241)	(220)	(303)	(227)	(991)
	Minus RMA	(194)	(3,622)	(4)	(1)	(3,821)
	Plus Shipment	720	360	-	240	1,320
	Delivered Shipments	-	720	360	-	1,080
	Ending Calculated Inventory	3,811	689	742	514	514
	Ending Reported Inventory	602	521	778	559	559
	Difference over (under)	3,209	168	(36)	(45)	(45)
	% Diff over Disti Reported Inv	533.06%	32.25%	-4.63%	-8.05%	-8.05%

Fig. 9.2. Data reconciliation example

also conducted a regular monthly data review with Zyme's head of operations, Ted Dimbero, with Sankaran, and with the customer's CFO. It was during these meetings that Zyme forwarded suggestions about additional reports and services to the customers.

Every so often, a customer requested a one-off special analysis. For example, two Zyme employees had jointly advised a customer on how to implement regular reporting at its distributors. The Zyme team flew around the world on their client's behalf, visiting their distributors and convincing them to execute the reporting. This was a 90-day project. While Zyme's weekly reports were not charged separately, customers were willing to pay additionally for one-off analyses like these. It remains to be seen whether this sort of dedicated service would generate significant revenues over time.

Zyme had worked out a pricing policy low enough not to be a deterrent to the customer, but sufficiently high to allow Zyme a positive margin from even small volume customers. A fixed monthly fee covered setup costs. Theoretically, Zyme reserved the right to vary the fixed fee with the complexity of the client's requirements, but until mid-2006, they had not found it necessary to exercise this right. The additional fee was based on the number of data sources, but with a decreasing marginal price, and there was a separate fee for a three-month one-off special project.

9.1.3 The Back End: The Outsourced Bangalore Center

Zyme's operations center was located in Bangalore, India. All data collection and consolidation – invisible (and, in a way, irrelevant) operations to the client – took place there. Zyme had an exclusive agreement with a large Indian business process outsourcing (BPO) provider. The BPO staffed the center to Zyme's specifications and executed operations with its existing IT infrastructures. The BPO was paid $8 per employee per hour (although analysts were paid a monthly salary), earning a margin of 50%.

Zyme's service package included well-trained people and technology. In December 2005, the operations center had about 30 people, who were organized by client-specific operations teams. A large client would have a team of five or six, a smaller client one or two people. Each team had a senior team leader who knew all process steps in detail and had analysis and reporting skills. Eighty percent of the workforce consisted of junior analysts, 20% of whom performed only generic work, switching back and forth between two or three clients. Renison Correya, the manager of the operation, was an employee of the BPO, but had been working with Zyme for 2 years, since it introduced its first customer. He was connected to Ted Dimbero in the US by a weekly telephone meeting, and to each individual CSM by daily instant messenger communications. A bright 27-year-old, he was already carrying substantial management responsibility.

Dimbero had developed a test for the recruitment of new analysts that was adapted to the specific requirements of the sophisticated analysis work, including math, Excel, and pattern recognition. After passing the test and the interview, which was conducted by Zyme, a new recruit also had to go through certification both on Zyme's processes and on the client's business processes. Analysts continued to undergo weekly training sessions, job rotation, and best-practice sharing activities. Dimbero had a monthly telephone meeting with the entire operation center, and visited it once every quarter, occasionally represented by one of the senior CSMs.

The analysts found their work very interesting and enjoyable – there was no employee turnover at all, in marked contrast to the "normal" turnover of around 20% in a BPO organization. After a certain time, the operations team mastered the client's terminology and spoke the client's language, including the SKUs and the client's part numbers; they knew the distributors by name, and were knowledgeable about the customer's quarter-end sales analysis and performance. The team acted as an extension of the client organization.

The CSM was responsible for the quality of the data, so during the early stage, the cleaned data were sent first to the CSM for a check, and then forwarded to the client. Once the process was stabilized (after two to six weeks, depending on the client), the analyst team worked independently. The team could handle the problems in the incoming files. Quality was rigorously checked with a 100% redundancy principle – all calculations were performed independently and simultaneously by two team members and then compared and discrepancies pursued. The results were sent directly back to the client, and copied to the CSM, who remained highly involved in the exception reports and business analysis.

9.1.4 Zyme's Own Bangalore Center

Zyme opened its own facility in Bangalore in December 2005 in order to bring key competences back in-house when its cash flow began to allow it. Sankaran recruited Sudhakar Joshi to head it. Joshi was an experienced facility support manager who had worked in both large and small companies. "The service quality in this company is great," he commented, "and it is my job to allow everyone to be productive in their work."

In January 2006, the facility's cubicles were still empty. By the end of 2006, the center housed 40 analysts employed by Zyme. The plan was that once sufficient volume had been reached, Zyme would pull the critical mass of analysis capacity, with its crucial expertise, back in-house, while continuing to work with the BPO.

The group had two teams: one business analyst team conducting more advanced analysis in addition to the analysis in the BPO center, and one engineering team developing supporting technology for Zyme's operating process. A three-person engineering team was working on automation, the technology component of its service package. This included the auto-forward process from the client to the operations center, and a standard template for transferring channel information that was sent out to all distributors. All files that arrived in the standard template format were read and written directly into an application that was capable of checking simple errors (for example, wrong format of an SKU) and of aligning the inventory and pricing terms in the files with the customer's fiscal calendar. However, only 70% of the distributors adhered to the standard template. The remaining 30% had to be processed manually (cut and pasted into the correctly formatted file).

The goal of the automation project was to reduce the manual double-checking work, and to improve data quality and scalability. Higher productivity also offered a hedge against an increase in Indian labor costs. As well as the automation work, the engineering team contributed its special expertise to provide additional ad hoc client services (30% of its time was given to this).

"We have an automation plan," commented Girish Elchuri, the engineering manager, "but it will take time to handle all the differences in format and content across customers and to build robustness, because distributors are not disciplined and provide low-quality data. This automation will incorporate a lot of specialized expertise – it's not a cheap quick job." Indeed, Zyme hoped that leveraging proprietary automation across clients (offering them economies of scale) would be a major and difficult to imitate advantage – customers were explicitly mentioning it as something they expected to emerge.

9.1.5 Impact on the Customer Organizations

Zyme had established its model and was building a reputation for service. Companies with far-flung indirect channels were beginning to consider outsourcing a function as business-critical as obtaining channel sell-through data. Customers found that once Zyme had proved the reliability of its processes, quality was faultless, flexibility in response to changes in customer processes very high, and the company continued to propose additional reports that increased its value further. As a result, customers inevitably ended up handing over data collection and reporting to Zyme, except for occasional accuracy checking with channel partners. This affected between five and ten employees at each customer.

However, although the work had been handed over, not a single job had been lost at any of the ten clients by April 2006. Instead, one customer observed that the employees had been "shifted to more value-added activities – rather than doing data entry and checking, we are now focusing on analysis. This means reporting, revenue forecasting, evaluating the effectiveness of marketing programs [through the effect on weekly sales], and interacting with the channel partners." Another said, "We are now doing analyses that we simply never performed before because our plates are always so full that we never got to them," a benefit corroborated by several other clients. Once Zyme's process was in place, several customers started to collect more data from the channel partners – not only sell-through but also end-user information and more detailed product information – which allowed better sales analyses and forecasting.

One customer used Zyme to track the effect of special promotions on sell-through and administering the incentive payments to the partners. "We could not have rolled out this program so widely *and* gotten out the payments *and* evolved our processes – IT resources and time would have been too scarce." Moreover, the analysts clearly found the new work more interesting, and as a result a reduction in turnover among these channel tracking groups was reported by several clients.

Can we conclude from this that through off-shoring Zyme created jobs for both the US and the Indian economies (40 in Bangalore – 35 at the BPO partner and five internally – and 15 in the US by late 2005, with rapid growth for the foreseeable future) without eliminating any jobs at their client companies? An off-shoring skeptic might counter that although no jobs were directly lost, a more subtle employment drain was at work: the creation of new jobs within client companies was prevented as Zyme grew, because Zyme scaled the channel tracking work for them. One San Francisco Bay area client described the effects of this: "I had eight people before in my channel tracking group, six of whom have been redeployed to higher-value activities. But as we scaled channel programs up, I would have had to increase my group to 20 people in order to handle the volume, and we could avoid that because Zyme helps us. Thus, we are leveraging our people better. Without Zyme, we would have had to invest in expensive and inflexible automation, or created some jobs in Oregon, where wages are not as expensive as in California." Does this imply that jobs were retained in California but that potential jobs had in effect moved from Oregon (or other lower wage areas in the US) to India?

The answer is not straightforward. First of all, an important message from this client is that, unable to handle certain jobs within the main operation, they would have been obliged to look for a low-cost provider in any case, in order to remain competitive. Yet, extending this to support the argument that off-shoring is an inevitable consequence of competition does not do justice to the full effect of Zyme's activity. In another customer's words, "The better data quality produced with Zyme's help allows us to look further ahead, to see pricing inconsistencies and to see sales numbers from end customers, not only from distributors. This would be a huge win. We would be able to respond to end-customer demand directly, and we would become capable of compensating behavior by our channel partners, not only results. Although indeed a couple of analyst jobs were not created in the short run because of Zyme, better channel management will allow us to grow more, and therefore, ultimately, we will hire more people." Thus, strategically aware clients used Zyme not defensively, to cut costs, but proactively, to increase value creation. Their experience and expectation was that higher value creation would boost economic activity and create jobs.

9.1.6 Next Steps for Zyme

Revenues in 2006 reached over $2 million. At the end of 2006, Zyme took the next step: it expanded the idea of cleansing, structuring, modeling, analyzing and interpreting complex data to other fields, and the channel sales data analysis became one business unit, led by Ted Dimbero. The customer trusted Zyme to perform the data management service for risk and insurance exposure modeling, and the next target was to do the same in the field of customer intelligence. Zyme's innovative business model was well positioned for success and expanded during 2007.

Is this too good to be true? Does Chandran Sankaran's success sound too much like the story of the alchemist who tried to turn lead into gold? Let's look at another example, where a British company's announcement that it was moving its manufacturing off-shore led to large-scale redundancies, national outrage, and questions raised in the House of Commons.

9.2 James Dyson and the Philosopher's Stone

Until 2002, James Dyson was regarded as one of Britain's iconic business figures, having made a huge personal fortune and raised the profile of British inventiveness with his innovative household technologies, which transformed the design and functioning of vacuum cleaners and washing machines. That year, however, he announced that he would be moving vacuum-cleaner manufacturing off-shore to Malaysia, with the loss of 800 jobs in the UK. A further 65 jobs were lost the following year when washing-machine manufacture was also transferred. The fury of workers at the plant in Malmesbury, the headquarters of Dyson in the UK ("He has betrayed British manufacturing and British consumers who have put him and his product where it is today") was echoed in the British media. The Prime Minister, Tony Blair, faced questions in parliament about the loss of British jobs overseas. City commentators, however, were more sanguine about the news.

Malmesbury is a small town with a population of 4 500 in the south of England. Many workers commuted to the Dyson plant from the Midlands and southwest. It was not the obvious place to site a major manufacturing operation but James Dyson was committed to the area. Only 2 years before his decision to close down UK manufacturing, he had applied for planning permission to extend the Malmesbury plant in order to increase production (permission was refused by the local council). The 800 redundancies at Dyson hit the community particularly hard, as they followed the layoff of 600 workers from Lucent Technologies, a US company, the previous year. The town's mayor, John Bowen, while angered at the company's decision, recognized its necessity: "One only has to look at the economic situation and realize that it was almost an inevitable fact. The one positive thing is that research and development will be staying and one hopes that with the new markets reopening in America, that might mean more jobs."

Dyson himself acknowledged his *volte face* in an interview with the BBC: "It's been an agonizing decision and very much a change of mind." However, manufacturing in Malaysia was much cheaper and, just as importantly, brought the company closer to its suppliers and new, growing markets.

> Increasingly in the past 2 or 3 years our suppliers are Far East based and not over here. And our markets are there too. We're the best selling vacuum cleaner in Australia and New Zealand, we're doing well in Japan and we're about to enter the US. And we see other Far Eastern countries as big markets as well.

Nevertheless, engineering union leaders saw the move as meaning only one thing: "This latest export of jobs …is confirmation that his motive is making even greater profit at the expense of UK manufacturing and his loyal workforce. Dyson is no longer a UK product."

The furor over Dyson's move to off-shoring put him on the defensive – yet it was not a knee-jerk, cost-cutting operation; it was a decision founded on a strategic refocusing of the company's activities: "Making R&D the top priority is the best blueprint for the renaissance of invention and engineering in Britain."

During 2001–2002, Dyson had invested £38 million in research and development. In 2005 alone the sum invested in R&D was £50 million and projected investment during 2006 was £60 million. Employment in the Malmesbury center increased to 1,200, with jobs created for 420 additional scientists, engineers, and technicians. In April 2006, Dyson was awarded the Queen's Award for Enterprise for outstanding growth and success overseas. Asked to comment, he said:

> Two years ago we were exporting one third of our vacuum cleaners. Today it's two thirds. The success is due to hard and intelligent work by the people working here in Malmesbury and of course, a growing overseas team. We have a relentless appetite for new and better technology. That's why we're taking on more and more engineers.

Off-shore production had resulted in increased profits that were fed back into the UK economy, leading to major investment in research and associated jobs. It was what Dyson and the City had wanted to see happening: within 2 years Dyson had become the best selling vacuum cleaner in the US, western Europe, Australia – and even Japan. Off-shoring had led not just to the cost-cutting needed to maintain performance, but to increased competitiveness and job creation. As one commentator put it: "Cost savings can go either to the customer or into improving the product – and that research is all done in Britain. It's much more valuable, and a good deal more interesting, than merely putting the bits together."

In other words, not just jobs, but "better" jobs. Zyme's clients noticed the same thing: off-shoring elements of their work that their people found dull and frustrating revitalized their employees' effectiveness and commitment. This touches on the complex issue of the nature of the work that feeds a community and an economy. What are the social implications of the exchange of "intelligent work" for manual labor? How should employers, local communities, educationalists, governments – social systems – prepare for this kind of development at both local and national levels? What happens to the people who could be "putting the bits together"? Is it always wise or desirable to turn base metal into gold? Is this the downside of the philosopher's stone? We will look at some of these issues in the next section.[2]

9.3 The "Does Off-Shoring Destroy Jobs?" Debate

9.3.1 The Evidence

The Zyme and Dyson examples relate to a fiercely conducted debate in Europe: perhaps the "capitalists" create jobs, but where are those jobs located? In an era of globalization and off-shoring, the jobs are created not in Europe but in developing countries, where employees – not just laborers but highly qualified engineers – work longer hours, accept lower wages, and are in some cases as competent as those in Europe (or the United States, for that matter). According to the anti-globalization activists who protest at G7 summit meetings, globalization is the arch enemy of the wealth of a normal person living in Europe.

Is this true? Existing evidence does not support the claim of whole-scale job movement, at least not across the board. When we consider aggregate job statistics, we simply cannot find lost jobs. They are a mirage. Consider the counter-acting forces in Fig. 9.3. On the one hand, moving factories and call centers off-shore and redirecting investments into the East means the shifting of jobs (left-hand side of Fig. 9.3). On the other hand, as industries, and therefore economic activity,

 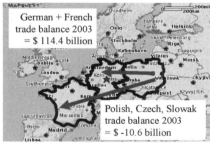

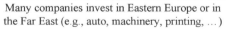
Many companies invest in Eastern Europe or in the Far East (e.g., auto, machinery, printing, …)   … but successful exports also create jobs.

Fig. 9.3. Positive and negative effects of off-shoring on jobs

---

[2] Sources: *Daily Telegraph* August 28, 2003; BBC News February 5, 2002, www.dyson.co.uk, www.thisiswiltshire.co.uk February 6, 2002.

wealth, and markets, develop in the East, large markets emerge for European countries, as reflected in large positive trade balances. A positive trade balance in France means that a job that could have been performed in Poland (because the resulting good was consumed there) was, in fact, performed in France. The huge exports from Western Europe imply job exports from the target markets into Western Europe (right-hand side of Fig. 9.3). The total effect is unclear at the level of the individual economies, but we can conclude that the claim that jobs are being exported wholesale out of Europe is unjustified.[3]

What we *can* derive from macroeconomic statistics is the benefit of trading: those countries that open their borders to trade and competition grow more. Countries that close their borders first enjoy a short-lived advantage from their protectionism but soon thereafter suffer stagnation and fall behind other, more dynamic economies.[4]

However, not everyone enjoys the benefits of globalization, trade, and off-shoring equally. Just like technological progress, off-shoring represents a positive sum game with a net benefit, but there are winners and losers. The losers are the same for both technology and labor mobility: those in low-qualified occupations. Low-qualified jobs have lost out in the dynamics surrounding supply and demand for labor. For example, the supply of low-skilled labor has decreased in Europe; the average amount of schooling increased in Germany from 9.5 years in 1970 to 13.5 years in 1998, and similar trends held in all OECD countries. The ratio of low-educated workers (below secondary education) to highly educated workers (at least some tertiary education) decreased from 3.6 to 1.3 in the United Kingdom and from 6.6 to 2.7 in France between the early 1980s and mid 1990s.[5]

Although the fraction of low-skilled workers has decreased, demand for un-skilled labor has decreased even more (Fig. 9.4). Technology advances statistically explain 50% of reduced demand, because they make the highly skilled more productive through new applications, while automating low-skilled jobs. The effect of technology is twice as great as the effect of off-shoring in the sense that highly skilled jobs remain in Europe because of (still) superior education, specialization, closeness to customers, and ability to direct others, whereas low-skilled jobs are being replaced by cheaper labor in developing countries. The remaining 25% of demand reduction for low-skilled labor may be explained by a host of other factors.[6]

---

[3] This analysis holds for most developing markets, with the exception of China because of its very strong exports in a few labor-intensive industries, such as textiles. The effect of exports is somewhat diminished but not entirely negated, because exports include more sub-components produced in developing countries. This effect can be measured according to the percentage of manufacturing value added in the exports (see Bergoeing et al. 2004).

[4] Paul Krugman has written extensively on this point; see Krugman (1997) or visit the Web page http://web.mit.edu/krugman/www/#fortune.

[5] See De la Fuente and Domenech (2000) and Strauss-Kahn (2003).

[6] See Feenstra and Hanson (1999), Strauss-Kahn (2003) and the *Economist* (2007d).

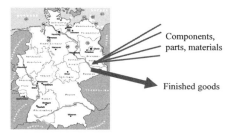

Components,
parts, materials

Finished goods

Technology:	**Outsourcing:**
• Automation of routine jobs	("vertical specialization")
• Productivity increase of highly qualified jobs (e.g., analyses, information access)	• Completion of different production stages in differing countries with international transport of parts
• New opportunities and businesses	• Move unskilled labor-intensive activities into less developed countries with lower costs
50 %	**25 %**

Fig. 9.4. Technology and off-shoring reduce the demand for unskilled labor

As a result of these supply-and-demand effects, pressure on low-skilled occupations increases. In the US and the UK, this pressure results in relative wage reductions; the fraction of US national income earned by the top percentiles has increased, and the ratio of minimum wage to median wage deteriorated from 0.45 to 0.36 between 1980 and 2000. Wage regulation has prevented relative wages from changing as much in Europe – in France, the ratio of minimum to median wage *increased* from 0.57 to 0.61 in the same time frame – but employment demands have shifted to more skilled jobs, and unemployment has increased, mainly among unskilled laborers.[7] In addition, low-skilled workers have seen their real wages shrink in the last decade in spite of wage protection.[8]

In short, low-skilled members of society are right to be worried about the effect of technology and globalization on them. And they clearly are worried, which leads to resistance to reforms and fringe-voting in elections.[9] Society has a responsibility to provide them with an education that allows as many of them as possible to compete in the more sophisticated labor market, and to ease their transition to another occupation.

Surely, the conclusion drawn from the observation that low-skilled people are the losers in the offshore-and-trade game cannot be to stop trading and off-shoring or to slow down technological progress. Both these options lead to disaster, as extreme examples from history demonstrate. China was economically and technologically leading Europe by at least 150 years in 1,400 but then stopped progressing,

---

[7] Source: OECD Employment Outlook 2004 and 1997. Similar statistics hold for Germany.

[8] See Sauga et al. 2007.

[9] See Köcher 2007.

so that by 1,700, it had become so backward that it was exploited and looked down upon by Europeans. The country's backward progression came about largely because of the desire of the all-powerful central elite to stabilize and control everything and their lack of interest in trading with and learning from the West.[10] Similarly, the Soviet Union ultimately collapsed because it fell behind the Western bloc economically, partially as a result of central control and a lack of diversity, as well as the dearth of economic exchange.

More subtly, strong evidence suggests some European product and labor laws, meant to protect the vulnerable members of society who lack higher education, have turned out to have the opposite effect. Consider the analysis in Fig. 9.5, which shows the effect of one outsourced dollar on the entire economy in a comparison between the United States and Germany. Imagine a factory moves from Boston to India, and call the total spending 100% (or $1.00 in Fig. 9.5). The investment disappears from Boston, and many people lose their jobs. The effect is negative, maybe even devastating on the local community. But what is the effect on the economy as a whole? Do benefits exist that partially compensate for the loss? Consider the upper part of the figure.

First, *consumers gain.* In the overall economy, US consumers get 58 cents of the lost dollar back in the form of savings. This figure represents real and significant wealth: we buy shoes, clothes, computers, or white goods much more cheaply than we could previously because they are made in the Far East, which literally

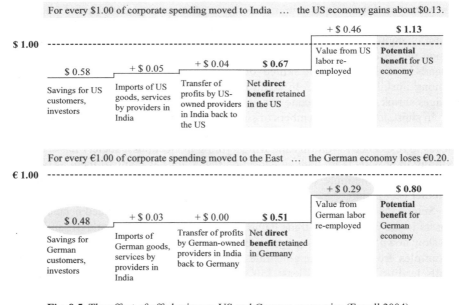

Fig. 9.5. The effect of off-shoring on US and German economies (Farrell 2004)

---

[10] A good overview is given by Mokyr (1990, chapter 9).

puts more money in the consumer's pocket. The shareholders of the company earn a small portion of the 58 cents, because it retains some cost savings.

Second, small gains occur because the added economic activity in India draws some export products from the United States (5 cents) and because some Indian companies owned (partially) by US companies profit from the added economic activity (4 cents). In total, the US economy gains 67 cents of the lost dollar back directly because of the effects of cheaper production. But these figures still fail to take into account that the unemployed workers (and managers) and empty buildings will not simply remain idle; they find other jobs and other uses. Redeploying equipment and workers into *other productive occupations* provides another big source of regaining value (46 cents).

In sum, an unexpected picture develops. Although $1 was lost, seemingly disappearing from the economy, in the end the US economy wins $1.13 back for a net benefit. Thus, we conclude that in this scenario, *off-shoring activity has win–win potential both for the Indian and U.S. economies*: India wins because it gains employment and economic activity, and the US economy wins because it reaps the benefit of lower costs and can redeploy production factors (capital and people) to other, more productive and/or innovative uses. This situation represents nothing other than an instance of the law of the benefits of trade: both economies specialize and trade, and as a result, the entire system (across countries) becomes more productive. Remember, productivity drives growth.

Figure 9.5 contrasts the US economy's net benefit from off-shoring with the effect of the same off-shoring decision on the German economy (bottom part of Fig. 9.5). Again, €1 is lost to India, and equipment and workers fall idle. The study claims that the German economy wins only 80 cents of this €1 back and suffers a net loss from off-shoring. Why? Because of *product* and *labor market rigidities* (both shaded). First, the German consumer gains only 48% (not 58%) from off-shoring because prices do not go down as much as in the U.S economy: taxes, zoning laws, business hour restrictions, price regulations, and a host of other regulations reduce competition and prevent efficiencies from being passed on to the consumer.[11] Second, less labor and capital gets redeployed, so the economy gains back only 29 cents (instead of 46 cents). Strong job protection and high social charges make companies reluctant to hire, so they rely more on automation and temporary work.

However, other more complete studies suggest that the picture in the lower half of Fig. 9.5 is much more positive in Germany as well. There are many motives for off-shoring, and it turns out that the majority of companies, at least in Germany, pursue it to develop new markets and access talent, rather than just saving costs.[12] Studies both in the US and Germany show that the companies that off-shore for the development of new markets tend to increase employment at home – in other words, in the majority of cases, employment is created even at the level of the individual company.

---

[11] Lewis (2004) and Jørgensen (2005).

[12] Buch and Schnitzer 2007, pp. 47 and 52.

At the level of the economy, off-shoring (or more generally, foreign direct investment by German companies) in Western countries clearly increases employment in Germany, and even off-shoring in Eastern Europe and the Far East does not (statistically) reduce employment in Germany.[13] Moreover, the presence of foreign direct investment in an economic sector does *not* reduce wages in that sector – the jobs that are created at home when work is moved abroad tend to more highly skilled and more highly paid (as we discussed earlier). In other words, market expanding off-shoring outweighs cost-reducing and job-shifting off-shoring in Germany, and as a result, the results for the economy overall are more positive than negative. The message from the overall economic data is clear – compared to Fig. 9.5, the picture is more complete as all off-shoring activities are considered, not only the cost-reduction driven shift of one job from the high-wage country to a low-wage country.

9.3.2 Implications for Companies and Policy Makers

After reviewing the evidence on the impact of off-shoring, we arrive at the conclusion that companies' key responsibility for the economy lies in achieving and sustaining (global) competitiveness, which requires restructuring and change as industries track the turbulent demands of the world economy. Two important vehicles for achieving change, technology advancement and off-shoring/outsourcing, are both necessary and inevitable in the drive toward specialization and productivity enhancements that produce wealth. This results, however, in turbulence and parties that lose at the local level. Society needs to produce opportunities that can be offered to the losers of restructuring in the short term.

Off-shoring is often discussed in the press as a cost reduction measure, and 50% of managers in INSEAD's executive seminars view it that way. However, there are broader reasons for off-shoring.

- It can unlock additional "extended capacity" that helps buffer demand variations: in a high-demand season, a flexible plant, say, in Eastern Europe, can make additional volume of a product.
- It is a way to understand and/or address new markets: for example, one winner of the 2007 Industrial Excellence Award, the small company Wemhöhner that makes wood paneling machines with just 300 employees, opened an assembly and sales office in China in order to tap into the rapidly growing Chinese market.
- It can provide access to talent. For example, we have talked to several European companies recently who were building R&D centers in Eastern Europe, India and China because they were not able to find qualified engineers in Europe – the market for talent here was swept clean.

---

[13] Buch and Schnitzer 2007, pp. 137, 147.

- It can provide access to scientific or market related knowledge. For example, the Japanese NTT Docomo has an R&D center in Munich in order to be informed about the European telecommunications market. East Asian universities and research centers are rapidly upgrading and climbing up the international rankings – just think of the cutting edge expertise on tropical and diseases that has recently emerged in India.

- Finally, it can give a company access to new capabilities. Coming back to Zyme Solutions, software companies in India (for example, around Bangalore) are world leaders in software development processes and outsourcing contracting and systems for project delivery. Companies place centers in Bangalore not to save costs (for facilities and managers in Bangalore, the cost is as high as in California), but to get access to world-class processes.

The lesson for companies is that the narrow use of off-shoring merely for cost savings is defensive and, while it is not disappearing, it is becoming an increasingly incomplete view of off-shoring. The best companies use off-shoring proactively as a strategic weapon along multiple dimensions. To illustrate this, we come back to the competitiveness diamond that we introduced in Chap. 1: Fig. 9.6 shows that off-shoring can support a company in all the strategic position games: on the left, access to talent and knowledge for innovation and differentiation, on the right access to expanded markets, and at the bottom, access to partners and extended capabilities.

For example, through its investment in Dacia in Romania, Renault increased sales in Eastern Europe (and in France, with the Logan model), adding jobs in the French headquarters and engineering center. Volkswagen is enhancing its R&D

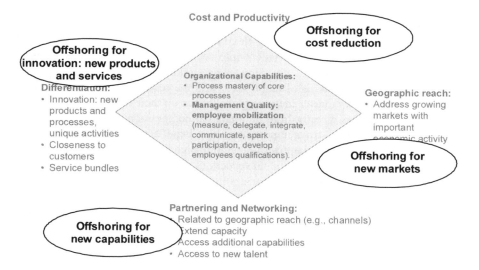

Fig. 9.6. Off-shoring as a strategic weapon rather than just a cost-cutting measure

activities in China, which will allow the company to develop more car models and create at least a few jobs in Germany. Partnerships between European and Indian pharmaceutical companies have helped Europeans with drugs developed from substances of which they were previously unaware.

Utilized in this broader way, off-shoring becomes a strategic weapon with much higher value creation potential. And used in this way, off-shoring creates employment rather than suppressing it. Recall the evidence shown in Chap. 1 (Fig. 1.1): industry growth requires growth of the most successful companies, and as we will see in Chap. 10, there is evidence that if the companies are successful, there is a positive "spiral effect."

However, we have also seen that off-shoring creates winners and losers in society, and most of the losers are the less educated. This macro-economic effect holds lessons for policy makers and politicians. The conclusion is not that European countries should simply reduce protection of this group to allow unimpeded progress (despite claims that "workers are too coddled and must lose privileges in the interest of the economy" from the business side in this debate). It is not in anyone's interest to exclude a class of the population from wealth. Not only does it run against democratic principles, but removing all prospects from a population group leads to upswings in the political right wing and unrest (e.g., the burning of 10,000 cars in Paris and Marseilles at the end of 2005). The challenge thus becomes to support the most vulnerable members of society by helping them change with the economic system and buffering them from changes they cannot manage, without blocking (and perhaps even while supporting) this economic change.

The macro-economic benefits of off-shoring are well known. In the words of Buch and Schnitzer (2007, p. 162), the implications for politicians can be summarized as follows: "Governments should certainly not restrict the activities of internationally active companies. However, companies, markets and regions are heterogeneous; some reduce employment while others expand it. Therefore, markets and employees need to be sufficiently flexible to enable mobility from sectors and companies with shrinking employment into sectors and companies that expand. This requires, in addition to supporting labor market conditions, flexibility, and high qualifications and skills of employees. It is the responsibility of the state to help those who cannot master these new challenges on their own. Protecting companies and employees directly from international competition, in contrast, is not a sensible strategy, as it destroys important welfare benefits of globalization."

This book complements the macro-economic picture by showing that the benefits also exist at the level of individual successful companies. This holds important lessons for managers: your first responsibility to society is achieving competitiveness; you are not destroying jobs in the long run by achieving competitiveness. Competitiveness rests on management quality and strategic positioning, which have many dimensions besides off-shoring as we have demonstrated throughout this book. However, you need to keep the effects of your actions on your surrounding communities in mind and reach out when you can. Stop complaining about politicians and unions; instead, start engaging with them for win-win solutions. That is the topic of the last chapter.

Chapter 10

Accountability for Competitiveness, Collaboration for Jobs

In this chapter, we discuss some implications that managers and policy makers may draw from the examples and observations in this book. We have started our line of evidence with the observation that the management teams of industrial firms bear the responsibility for making their firms competitive – through management quality, or the ability to mobilize the workforce, and by adopting promising strategic positions (summarized in the competitiveness diamond in Chap. 1). The case studies in Chaps. 2 through 9 have demonstrated that all the positions in the diamond are feasible in Germany and France. We have finally shown that off-shoring, the practice of performing certain activities abroad in low-wage or industrialized countries, does not deserve its bad reputation as "job killer." On the contrary, off-shoring tends to create value, growth and jobs; this is the case in the excellent companies that we have showcased in this book, who use it strategically rather than just as a cost-cutting tool, and job creation is also observed by systematic studies at the level of the economy. There are challenges, however, which include job churn, training and potential relocation. This book cannot fully discuss, much less solve, how these social issues can be addressed at governmental level. Our point is that management needs to step up to its part of the responsibility, and policy makers must recognize that it is their responsibility to help companies be competitive, not fight them or see them simply as cows to be milked for supporting needy parts of the economy. Finally, we argue that what seems to be missing in Germany and France today is an honest dialogue between the public sector and companies.

10.1 The Responsibility of Management

10.1.1 Responsibility for Competitiveness and the Market for Management

Chapters 2 through 9 showed excellent companies that are globally competitive. However, not all companies succeed in achieving competitiveness, of course. Germany saw spectacular failures, with Holzmann and KirchMedia, for example, and France has seen similar failures with companies like Alstom. Germany, in particular, perceived a management malaise at the beginning of the decade, and

German companies overall were undervalued in stock markets compared with other companies with the same sales, profits, and growth prospects.[1]

After a top management shake-up in many large German firms, the country saw great increases in the activities of private equity funds that buy, restructure, and sell companies. Takeovers by private equity funds were very controversial because they were perceived to lead to ruthless job losses and shifts to low-cost countries. A prominent politician coined the phrase "locust plague" to describe the raiding of the country by private investors. The example of Grohe often appeared in the press; the company was sold twice to investors, loaded with debt in the process, and then wanted to move a factory to Eastern Europe to cut its manufacturing cost. The reaction in France was similar – for example, the government declared a number of "strategic industries" that would not be allowed to fall into foreign hands. When the press caught wind of the fact that one of these strategic companies was the yogurt maker Danone, newspapers and commentators had a field day making fun of "fortress France."

It turns out that private equity funds, like off-shoring, have an undeservedly bad reputation for killing jobs. Let's consider the evidence. The levers that private equity funds use to boost the valuation of the firms that they buy go far beyond mere cost- and job-cutting. Figure 10.1 shows a value tree with the key drivers of valuation; the levers influence valuation by the financial markets and improve business economics by influencing the return equation: (revenue – margins)/ capital employed.

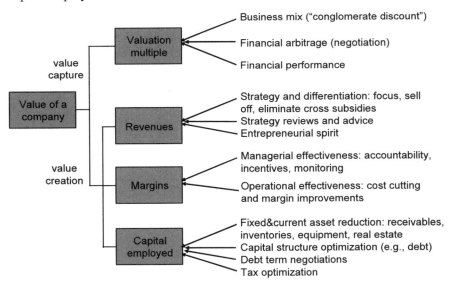

Fig. 10.1. What private equity investors do[2]

---

[1] See the *Economist* (2005).

[2] See Berg and Gottschalg (2003).

Financial arbitrage (out-negotiating the seller) and financial engineering (loading the company with debt and negotiating debt terms) represent two of these value levers, but the public discussion about private equity has tended to concentrate on them exclusively – perhaps because they make for "juicy stories" that confirm cynical suspicions.

Less often discussed is the fact that private equity companies also pursue true value creation, using several value levers. First, the investor team typically cleans up the business mix, focusing on a core set of related activities. This allows better management and raises valuation simply because the stock markets nowadays value focus (there is a conglomerate discount in the stock market, reversing the fads of the 1980s). The restructuring team also puts a priority on improving financial performance rapidly. Cost-cutting and efficiency improvements make the firm competitive, and although they sometimes eliminate jobs, they also create the foundation for a sound business that can then attack and grow again. Using experienced business experts, the investor improves the strategic positioning of the firm, which often means shedding loss-making peripheral activities that have accumulated because of a lack of management discipline. Insufficiently effective management changes and, in many cases, the culture and spirit of the organization actually improve because changes for the better, which may have been blocked previously, become possible.

This discussion implies that private equity, combined with the threat of takeovers by fast growing firms from newly developing countries, represents a useful pressure on firm management: if you do not manage the firm to achieve competitiveness (i.e., if you underperform to the extent that markets undervalue you), your company may be taken over, and you will be forced out because your underperformance represents an opportunity for others to do better and create value. Thus, management teams sense the pressure to upgrade, and even boards feel the pressure – as one investment banker commented, "Nobody feels safe, from Eon and Siemens downwards."[3] Indeed, companies brought back to the stock market after a restructuring by private equity investors are more successful than other stock market entrants,[4] and overall, private equity investments boost company growth and investment returns, for example, for national pension funds.[5] After the sub-prime crisis in the second half of 2007, private equity takeovers have diminished because the raising of capital has become more difficult, not because there are no opportunities left to improve the performance of management teams.[6]

Competitiveness demands performance improvements not only from employees but also from management. Senior managers have subtle tools to protect themselves, but takeovers and private equity provide additional economic levers that may expose top management to competition, a secondary correcting mechanism if supervisory boards fail. Top management must face this competition, but asking

---

[3] As quoted in Milne (2006).

[4] See Cao and Lerner 2006, *Economist* 2007 b.

[5] See *Economist* 2007c.

[6] Politi and Guerrera 2007.

for protection remains widespread, as shown by the rescue of Philip Holzmann, mentioned earlier, and the (now in the process of being repealed) "VW law" (which gives the state government minority blocking rights on VW's supervisory board) in Germany, the protection of Alstom and active government support of Sanofi's takeover of Aventis in France, or the 2002 steel tariff increases in the United States.

Companies commonly accuse governments of interfering with markets, but when they are threatened, they call for the very same interference. Of course, this temptation may be irresistible, but we must recognize that going to the government for help and protection when times get rough is anti-competitive.

10.1.2 Firms' Contribution to Society: Spillovers

Section 1.1 has again reiterated our earlier conclusion that the responsibility of firms to the economy and society is to face competition at the level of the organization and management. Firm competitiveness in an industrial sector provides the foundation for national competitiveness, as depicted in Fig. 10.2.

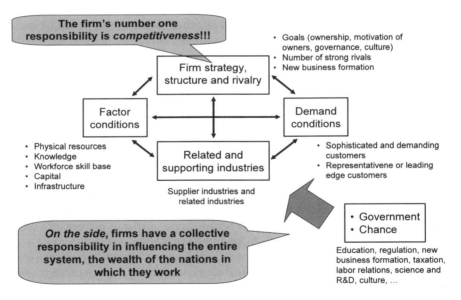

Fig. 10.2. Responsibilities of company management[7]

---

[7] This figure is based on Porter's (1990, pp. 70–127) industry competitiveness of nations diamond.

Consider the competitiveness diamond of Chap. 1 (Fig. 1.3) as the detailed structure of the upper box (firm strategy, structure and rivalry) in Fig. 10.2. Figure 10.2 highlights the interaction between firm competitiveness and the surrounding economy: firms influence the attractiveness of factor, industry, and market conditions.

Countries with abundant natural resources have an obvious advantage (e.g., Norway and the Arab peninsula from oil, Brazil from metals). However, if natural resources are not accompanied by competitive industries, sophisticated customers who push producers to perform, and the active expansion of a skilled workforce, they leave the country poor in the long run.

Furthermore, competitive firms represent the foundation of a competitive nation because they produce "spillovers." That is, a competitive industry, in which vigorous rivals compete with one another, spawns supplier industries (e.g., automotive suppliers, equipment suppliers for chip and computer manufacturers) and complementary industries of related products (e.g., communication devices that follow the opportunities created by wireless networks and the Internet). When a country achieves wealth and competitive clusters, the sophistication of its industries and population pressures industrial clusters to perform at their highest levels (see Fig. 10.2).

In addition to producing economic wealth and spillovers, firms should engage in support of their communities, not just because of a moral obligation but because it is good business. Community support advances the virtuous spiral in which people surrounded by wealth and sophistication want to do even better. Consider the manganese smelter company RDME featured in Chap. 8. RDME constructively manages it relationships with the local community, actively contributes to community life, and supports projects in the town of Grande-Synthe. In December 2003, RDME received the Grande-Synthe Prize for being one of the most dynamic and innovative companies in the district, in honor of its new activities, job creation, and community support. Good community relationships can be rewarding in and of themselves, as well as motivating, but they may also improve business: it is worth repeating from Chap. 8 that after restarting its furnace, RDME encountered some problems with increased smoke discharging into the atmosphere, but thanks to its permanent and transparent management of environmental issues, as well as continuous and voluntary relationships with local authorities, RDME received additional notice, which enabled the company to explain the measures it had taken to ameliorate the discharge.

Our older readers may feel a sense of *déjà vu* after reading this section: the early 1970s saw a public and economic mood swing from capitalism to a view that companies were responsible for creating wealth in the economy. As one of our older colleagues put it, "in the socialist era around the 1970s, companies were supposed to do everything. That proved unsustainable, and as a result 15 years later, we ended up with a rampant lack of competitiveness. The 1980s swung back toward capitalism and now we are swinging back again." Perhaps we are going through mood swings. However, the economic evidence does give clear guidance:

the first responsibility of companies is competitiveness (within the law and ethics). Then, companies need to be good citizens to the maximum extent possible, in order to mobilize solidarity and motivate employees.

We conclude this section by observing that, despite the limitations described, European companies can and are competing successfully globally. Examples of successful European companies abound in all industries – chemicals, electrical goods, power distribution, machine tools, cars, electronics, software, white goods, banks, specialty materials, pharmaceuticals, cosmetics, and alternative energy production, to name but a few. And in all sectors, Europe has at least several worldwide leaders. The more severe problems lie in the public sector.

10.2 The Contribution of Governments and Unions

This section addresses portions of the governments' and unions' challenges for job and wealth creation. Doing full justice to these complex issues is beyond the scope of this book: we focus on aspects that are close to the interaction between government, unions and businesses, which leads to the importance of a functioning dialogue among these partners, discussed in the next section.

10.2.1 The Government's Responsibility for Product and Labor Markets

The government has a significant influence on the industry competitiveness diamond (Fig. 10.2) through its provision of an infrastructure and its role in safeguarding property rights, as well as through regulations (such as the product and labor restrictions that we have discussed in Chap. 9), social charges and taxation, and the provision of public goods (especially the educational system). Two important areas of government influence have already been discussed in Chap. 9: the limited ability of the German (and other European) economies to offset restructuring and thus benefit from labor movements. The reasons in all cases go back to the lack of product market and labor market flexibility.

Clear evidence by now shows that product market restrictions, such as zoning laws, price restrictions, or selective subsidies, tend to reduce competition and lead to lower efficiency, productivity, and growth. Governments should therefore refrain from micromanaging. Although the temptation to achieve immediate benefits from correcting individual incidents is great, the indirect costs to the economy are typically underestimated. Competition-reducing regulation overall seems to have contributed to poorer growth in large European economies.[8]

---

[8] See Nicoletti and Scarpetta (2003).

The second major issue is labor market flexibility. The overprotection of jobs, even when well intentioned, has backfired and prevented many jobs from being created. Any loosening of job protection seems to prompt protest storms that make politicians wobble, for example, the De Villepin government in France backing down over youth job protection in 2006. And yet, examples of promising policies exist; consider the famous Danish "flexicurity" model.

Starting in the early 1990s, Denmark made it easier for companies to fire employees (though with notice and severance pay). In turn, workers receive generous unemployment benefits and other transitional help. After 2000, individuals who did not accept a job offer or actively seek employment or education saw their unemployment benefits sharply curtailed. In addition, they were required to join training courses, especially young people under the age of 25. At the most aggregate level, Denmark has performed spectacularly in recent years, with an economic growth rate of 3.5% in the first half of 2006 and unemployment of just 4%.[9]

However, the Danish model is one of the most expensive (5% of GDP in 2001), partially because in addition to the 4% unemployed, another 5% of the relevant population is engaged in education or transitional measures.[10] Therefore, some commentators assert that the problem has simply been pushed somewhere else, out of the public eye that is kept on unemployment statistics. Other criticisms come from all kinds of unexpected and creative directions. For example, some labor economists claim that the Danish model rests on a culture of "public spiritedness" (i.e., relatively low level of cheating the social system) and therefore cannot be applied in countries such as France or Italy.[11]

These dismissals of the Danish model seem unwarranted. Denmark has indeed experienced social cheating and therefore reduced the generosity of the system and tightened supervision and effort requirements for the unemployed after 2000. Moreover, cultural habits are less unchangeable than one might think – for example, French drivers were supposedly among the most inherently lethal in Europe, until (then) Interior Minister Nicolas Sarkozy radically increased fines and supervision in 2003, as a result of which traffic has slowed down systematically and the rate of accidents has decreased by half.[12]

Although the Danish model may not have reduced the total cost of unemployment, it has (along with decreases in product market rigidities and support for a positive business climate) emphatically contributed to economic success and growth and thus indirectly to a decreased unemployment burden on the economy and citizenry. Some of the effect is certainly due to the threat from losing benefits and thus inducing a higher incentive to look for work.[13] Moreover, the success of the Danish model has given citizens a higher general sense of security, in spite of

---

[9] According to the Economic Survey of the Danish Ministry of Finance, December 2006.

[10] See Westergaard-Nielsen (2001).

[11] See Algan and Cahuc (2006).

[12] The rate dropped from 184 to 90 road accident deaths per million inhabitants; Eurostat News Release 125, September 19, 2006.

[13] Handelsblatt 2007.

the objectively lower job security, and prevented feelings of exclusion. In contrast, in France, unemployment among 20–24 year-olds sits at 24% (versus 10% in Denmark or Germany), and an entire sector of the population feels excluded from opportunities. Riots and protests about the government's various attempts to tackle the situation through legislation have been frequent occurrences in France since late 2005. Finally, Denmark spends the highest amount of all countries on retraining (1.5% of GDP)[14] – in other words, one third of the total cost of the system is investment in skills rather than an expense.

The broader lesson is that unemployment represents a complex problem with many sources. The surest remedy against unemployment is economic growth, but managing unemployment requires a combination of labor market flexibility, support for the unemployed, and retraining schemes. Large countries are trying to attack the problem with centrally negotiated solutions among stakeholders with different interests, which seems increasingly ineffective – recall the transport strikes in France and Germany in October and November 2007. Governments instead must learn to allow decentralized experimentation, then compare experiences in other countries with experiments in their own states or provinces. The variety of insights provided by such experimentation offers the only hope of moving toward effective policies, with the awareness that any transfer of practices from one country or state to another requires modification and adaptation to local needs.[15] The same principle applies to complex innovations in companies, which come from decentralized experimentation and idea transfer.[16] Currently, the governments of large countries in Europe are failing in this challenge.

10.2.2 The Government's Responsibility for the Creation of New Firms

Although we have emphasized the responsibility of company management to create jobs in the economy, it is futile to expect a large number of jobs from large companies. By definition, large companies function in mature markets; they are big because they have grown over a long period and reached market saturation.[17] Companies in mature markets are subject to intense competition and consolidation, and they grow roughly with GDP (unless one firm takes market share from another) precisely because they are close to market saturation. But good companies still improve their productivity by 10% per year or more. We therefore arrive at the inevitable conclusion that large companies normally do not create many new jobs and at best maintain employment or grow slightly, not because they are ruthless capitalists but because market efficiency, competition, and productivity

---

[14] See *Economist* 2007.

[15] OECD (2006).

[16] See Loch and Kavadias (2007).

[17] See Utterback (1996).

improvements dictate it. Large established industries, such as pharmaceuticals, automobiles, chemicals, and machine tools, have slightly reduced their employment levels in the past decade.

Massive employment instead comes from new industries, such as the computer industry in the 1980s or the mobile phone and telecom industries in the 1990s. Consider a current example – the rapidly growing new industry in Germany, solar energy cells, already employs 150,000 people.[18] Start-ups and small companies make for volatile employers, in that most start-ups no longer exist after 5 years, so new companies create as well as destroy many jobs. However, more new companies are created in the US than in Europe, and even if many do not survive, new ones take their place, and new jobs tend to come from new firms entering markets.[19] The more dynamic firm creation environment in the US also has helped it take the lead in information technologies, the major growth-generating industry of the 1990s. Estimates suggest IT industries added 0.9% annual GDP growth in the US, compared with only 0.4–0.5% in Europe. This difference constitutes the lion's share of the growth difference between the US and Europe in the second half of the 1990s.[20]

The lesson for governments is to stop supporting failing firms in declining industries in a futile attempt to preserve jobs. Such efforts are not only extremely expensive but also ineffective in the medium to long term. The change of employment structure from manufacturing to services, and from less skilled to highly skilled job requirements, is inevitable; trying to prevent it makes the problems worse later on.[21] Instead, governments should foster competition to force mature and declining sectors to hold their own as much as possible while also retraining employees who have been made redundant, improving job placement services, and supporting those citizens who cannot retrain effectively. (Note that supporting them is often cheaper than keeping an entire industry alive, such as coal in Germany.)

A related implication of these observations is that governments should ease the regulations pertaining to new firm creation and simplify the costs and regulatory burden on young firms to help more of them survive. As we have pointed out, new firms create volatility in the job market, but if people can find new jobs and are supported in their efforts to do so, the psychological effect of volatility is less negative (as the experience in Denmark and other experiments shows).

After a new industry emerges, government must support its growth, for example, by helping it with its infrastructure needs. Governments have a poor track record of picking successful companies and industries before they arise (e.g., France's experience with Crédit Lyonnais and Japanese investments in MITI a decade ago), but once the new industry enters the growth phase, the government can and should support it. In the US, the IT industry enjoyed significant support in the second half

---

[18] See Kröher (2007).

[19] Brander et al. (1998) offer a detailed analysis for Canada and survey the corresponding results for the US.

[20] See Aiginger (2002) and Brander et al. (1998).

[21] *Economist* 2005b, Boston Consulting Group 2004.

of the 1980s, and alternative energy and environmental protection industries in Europe (especially Germany) are receiving such support now. Alternative energy industries might be the growth drivers for Europe in the next decade, just as IT was for the US in the 1990s. To maintain its lead, European industries require continued attention and investment in the face of a faster reacting US economy that can generate multi-billion dollar investments rapidly through its venture capital system.

10.2.3 The Government's Responsibility for the Education System

Education systems have traditionally been strong in Europe. Primary education is generally of high quality, and until recently European universities led the world. A well-educated workforce makes a critical contribution to economic competitiveness, and in this sense, the educational system must include continuous training over careers, as well as training of low-skilled individuals.

Large European countries have not invested enough in education and so have lost their leading position, as suggested by PISA studies of primary and secondary education. Moreover, the European universities have also fallen behind. A recent influential survey suggests that the top 50 universities include 39 North American, two Asian, five British, and four continental European institutions.[22] Although the level of research spending as a percentage of GDP is not markedly lower in Europe (e.g., 2.8% in the US, 2.6% in Germany, 2.2% in France in 2003), quality seems to be slipping from Europe, which has a direct effect on the economy, including a brain drain of the best and brightest people[23] and the relocation of company R&D facilities to locations near to top universities. Ambitions for university education in general have indirect effects as well.

The problem with European universities is not that they are public – there are multiple public universities among the top 50 (e.g., various University of California campuses) – it's that they *lack competition*. For example, the German government still considers it anti-social to let universities compete for students or students for universities (not to mention fees, which are hotly debated). In addition, because of their centralized policies, these institutes lack local experimentation, knowledge building, and specialized expertise accumulation, which means they depend completely on the wisdom of major decisions, which in turn leads to fragility and inertia. For example, the French government is reacting to university rankings by regrouping several leading social science labs to form a high-ranking social science

---

[22] The annual survey by the Institute of Higher Education, Shanghai Jiao Tong University, has caused some waves since its first appearance in 2003. The British institutes on the list are Cambridge (2), Oxford (10), Imperial College London, University College London, and Manchester; the Asian universities are Tokyo and Kyoto; and the continental Europeans are ETH Zurich (27), University of Utrecht (40), University Paris 06 (45), and Karolinska Institutet in Stockholm (50).

[23] See Saint-Paul (2004).

university. The German government has declared a few "elite institutions," to which it will provide extra funds in a strictly centralized procedure (which has set off complaints about micromanaging). Neither approach will produce innovative experimentation with the potential to lead eventually to significant performance improvements.

The rigidity of the French and German higher education systems creates a serious disadvantage. Although their systems produce a similar percentage of college-educated people as the US (if we include the apprenticeship ladder),[24] they require reform and modernization to remain relevant.[25] More investment in education systems is needed, but even more important are efforts to open them to diversity, local autonomy and experimentation, and competition.

The British system has been better in letting universities compete and giving money on the basis of performance (however imperfectly measured), and the comparatively stronger performance of the top British universities supports that direction. However, the British system works well only for the top universities and is relatively weaker in tertiary education of wider parts of the population: Britain seems to have a skill gap in the middle and in the population with vocational training.[26]

Improving the education of a large part of the population to give them up-to-date knowledge and the ability to solve sophisticated problems is one of the key ways of improving competitiveness and producing growth and jobs. The success of the Finnish economy is ascribed to their emphasis on R&D and investment in the education system.[27] Other European countries seem not to have given education the priority it deserves.

10.2.4 The Responsibility of Unions

Unions have played an overall constructive role in Europe since World War II by representing the interests of employees and contributing to all parts of the population that have participated in economic upswings. However, after a certain level of wealth has been achieved, the unions have tended to turn to short-term oriented defense of entitlements. During the simultaneous Thatcher era in the UK and Reagan era in the US, unions lost much of their power, but they retain critical power in the areas of collective wage bargaining in France and Germany (and hold 50% of supervisory boards in large companies in Germany).

---

[24] In Germany, 25% of the population has received tertiary education and 6% "other post-secondary" education; in France, this percentage is 32%; in the UK, it is 29%; and in the US, it is 38% (OECD *Education at a Glance* 2006).

[25] For a discussion of reforms of the German apprentice education system, see Müller (2006).

[26] See Stevenson 2007.

[27] Dutta and Larsen 2006. At the same time, however, large parts of the Finnish population continue to receive a low-quality education.

Bluntly, the unions have become an impediment to reform in France. French unions hold a simplistic view of companies as exploitative capitalists that must be opposed. One anecdote may serve as an example. During research for the Industrial Excellence Award, we visited a company that had bent over backwards to protect its employees from economic swings and let them share in the firm's success. We interviewed a representative of the workers' council (always a union member in France), who commented: "Well, I have to admit, although, of course, one can never really trust the bosses, that this management has been quite open in communication and seems to pursue a course that can benefit the workers ... Of course, I say this with the caveat that we are ready to see through any deception and strike quickly whenever there is a suspicion of a violation of duties." If the union is not willing to step out of its ideologically entrenched position, it cannot function as a partner and therefore hinders management effectiveness and competitiveness. As another example, consider the observation of a colleague serving on the supervisory board of a large French company: "The union representative on the board always says the same thing when we decide on something – like a parrot: 'I'm against!'"

Unions in Germany also retain ideological positions at central headquarters level, holding roles in centralized wage bargaining and membership of supervisory boards, and in both positions they hinder progress. At the same time, German unions have been much more pragmatic when working with companies, in some cases serving effectively as skeptical partners who question policy and force management to look for creative solutions that serve both competitiveness and workers.[28] We have seen many examples of worker councils (heavily influenced by unions) who worked with management to provide great working time flexibility – maintaining work time accounts that allow weekly working time to vary between 20 h and over 50 hs per week without overtime pay, as long as the long-term average remains close to legal working time limits. This sort of flexibility is very valuable to firms because it allows full utilization of expensive equipment, so increases the productivity of labor. We have rarely seen such flexibility and collaboration by unions in France.

The union's role as management's "tough partner" remains legitimate and constructive (reflecting real interest conflicts between owners and employees in "dividing the pie"), as long as all parties continue to seek win–win solutions. Strikes have been rare in Germany, averaging five lost working days per [year times 1,000 employees]. Only Austria (2.5 days) and six Eastern European countries have lower strike levels. France suffers from 16 days, the UK 35 days, and the Scandinavian countries between 40 and 50 days.[29]

---

[28] See Milne and Williamson 2006.

[29] According to the Federation of European Employers League Table of Strikes and Lockouts. Numbers are averages from 2002–2004. The six Eastern countries are Slovakia, Czechoslovakia, Russia, Latvia, Romania, and Hungary. The highest strike level is in Greece, with 580 lost days per [year times 1000 employees]. This includes "ceremonial" annual strike days in which a large part of the entire population participates.

However, unions continue to have a role to play in ensuring the engagement of employees and contributing to societal cohesiveness. They must resist the temptation of short-term protection at the expense of longer-term competitiveness and should openly explain this trade-off to their members, as they have failed to do thus far. The difficulty of working with unions contributes significantly to the massive investments of French companies abroad in recent years. The temptation of going for short-term successes is evident in Germany's labor negotiations in the spring of 2007 and in France and Germany in the fall of 2007: the unions want to cash in on the emerging economic recovery, running the danger of suffocating the upswing. Wanting a fair share of the pie is understandable, but we must not forget the total size of the pie.

However, a mirror argument applies on the employers' side. The emphasis in the public debate over the last 10 years has very much been on workers' concessions. While it is true that wage concessions have significantly increased Germany's competitiveness over the last decade, the result is that one group of the population in particular has lost out: dependent employees with medium to lower salaries have taken the brunt of the restructuring, seeing their real wages fall and, at the same time, their burden from social system contributions rise. They have suffered significant reduction in purchasing power. At some point, the discussion needs to turn from labor cost reductions to creating competitiveness from other sources; otherwise, the unions' arguments will gain weight, and social cohesion will suffer.

10.3 The Misguided Dialogue and the Public Debate

In Sects. 1 and 2 of this chapter, we set out the contributions that firms, governments, and unions must make to strengthen European competitiveness. From these recommendations, it becomes clear that *progress occurs only if at least these three stakeholders collaborate*. Such collaboration happens to various degrees in different countries of the EU, though the dialogue seems more active and fruitful in smaller countries (e.g., the Benelux and Nordic countries) than in larger ones. In the latter, the "dialogue" sometimes seems reduced to mutual accusations, as caricatured in Fig. 10.3. Although Fig. 10.3 is a caricature, it contains a grain of truth; we have heard many similar statements in private, off-the-record conversations.

Many senior managers with whom we have talked, particularly in France and Germany, are so frustrated by the handcuffs placed on them by unions and governments, which seem arbitrarily motivated by special interests rather than macroeconomic improvements, that they proclaim, "If they do not let us remain competitive here, we will invest only abroad from now on." Indeed, the number of firms moving out of Germany and France has increased,[30] and investment flows point in the same direction: foreign direct investments in France and Germany

---

[30] See Institut für Demoskopie Allensbach 2004.

Fig. 10.3. The misguided dialogue among stakeholders: parallel monologues

have fallen significantly recently, and France's investment outflows grew to twice the size of its inward investment flows in 2004.[31] Cynically, we might conclude that French industry has less confidence in the French environment than foreigners do. In Germany, foreigners seem to have lost confidence, in that foreign direct investment fell to a negative position in 2004 as foreign investors withdrew money from Germany.

However, fleeing the country or soldiering on by giving up economic partners at home is not a good idea in the long run. Firms need the respect and support of their communities to function; a hostile environment causes tangible friction in all transactions, which can harm business dramatically and in turn, backfire on society itself. All the signs indicate that the environment is turning even more hostile, that firms are indeed losing the public debate.[32] As McKinsey has observed, "Trust in NGOs, citizens' groups and online information sources has risen inexorably as faith in business – Enron, WorldCom – has declined."[33] A recent study in Germany concludes, "As senior managers have experienced a massive loss of credibility and are separated from the rest of society by a growing gap, they must prepare themselves for an increasingly hostile public that is critical of capitalism. Expected protests will be ideologically more diffuse than during the 1960s and 70s, but no less

---

[31] OECD *Observer* October 2005, OECD statistics, country statistical profiles 2006.

[32] Müller and Student 2006.

[33] Müller and Student 2006.

potent."[34] A recent poll in France also indicated that French citizens hate most, in order, George W. Bush, McDonald's, and bosses of large companies.

Firms cannot simply choose to fulfill their economic functions in an increasingly hostile climate. Instead, they must go on the offensive and educate the public – especially those citizens who do not understand the connection between competitiveness and employment. When shows on public television gleefully point to firms that maximize their share prices at the cost of the common worker by shedding jobs, firms must react and explain their choices and their long-term economic consequences. Concerted action by industry (perhaps helped by employers' associations) is required to prevent the hostility that stems from public misinformation.

In addition, firms must reach out to governments and unions. This is tricky at national level; although it worked in the Netherlands, it was more or less ineffective in Germany under Chancellor Gerhard Schröder. Instead, outreach should occur at local level (again, the example of RDME stands out here). If the firm is well respected in the local community as a constructive and honest partner, rhetoric at national level loses some of its impact, and degrees of freedom result.

A firm that does not manage its local relationships may repeat Hewlett-Packard's experience at its French headquarters: in 2005, the unions went to the streets, side by side with local politicians, to protest about the elimination of 1,240 jobs by the year 2008 (Fig. 10.4).

Labor undersecretary Gérard Larcher said that he "explained [to] the head of HP France that he regretted the brutal and unprepared character of the announcements, which affect both employees and communities."[35] The firm was publicly accused of cheating by first taking subsidies in a "labor protection contract" and then shedding the jobs. This accusation was later proved incorrect, but when local relationships sour, the cost of business increases.

Fig. 10.4. Jour de colère chez Hewlett Packard (Hate day at HP) (Source: TF1, September 16, 2005)

---

[34] Bonini et al. 2006.
[35] Television channel TF1, September 16, 2005.

Such public relations disasters continue to happen. Let's take an even more recent example from Germany: in January 2008, Nokia announced the pending closure of their mobile phone assembly plant in Bochum, a move that would shift 2,000 jobs (plus more in supplier companies) to Romania. This move came as big surprise to employees, unions and politicians. Employees duly expressed outrage, the German agriculture minister publicly switched to another phone brand, and the finance minister called this "caravan capitalism" (remember the locust metaphor that we discussed in Chap. 9?) and threatened a lawsuit to force Nokia to pay back subsidies they had received 2 years earlier, although this legal move has virtually no chances of succeeding.[36]

At the same time, German economists admitted that Nokia's move was justified: members of two respected economic analysis institutes pointed out that this was not surprising for the simple assembly jobs in the plant (considering that labor costs in Romania are 10% of those in Germany), and pointed out that Nokia was the last manufacturer still performing these jobs in Germany.

What is the lesson? Nokia's move may well be justified and inevitable. However, the firm failed to consult any of the stakeholders – we are not referring to asking permission, but to explanation, communication, and hearing people out. Thus, Nokia presented the stakeholders with a *fait accompli*, violating fair process. Their extremely negative reaction was the predictable result. By not acknowledging the need of the affected parties to be informed and heard (even if they have no decision right), firms systematically contribute to their negative image.

Firms must avoid a downward spiral of difficult business conditions that become more difficult because of mutual hostility. Such a spiral will hurt all sides, and a hostile environment in their own society will certainly hurt the firms involved.

10.4 Improving the Public Debate

A few principles of action emerge from our discussion in this chapter, which we summarize in Fig. 10.5. It is naïve to call these "recommendations," because the interests of the parties are sufficiently divergent to result in deeply different views of appropriate targets, their priority, and the causal effects of various actions. However, sufficient evidence exists to propose that if movement can be achieved on some of these items, the competitiveness and economic performance of European countries will improve. The capability for success in Europe undoubtedly exists; its managerial talent, infrastructure, innovation, and knowledge rank among the best in the world. What Europe now needs is the political and societal will to use its talents. If we do not exercise our talents, we run the all-too-real danger of becoming caught in a downward spiral.

---

[36] See Williamson 2008; Frankfurter Allgemeine January 17, 2008.

- Be competitive
  - strategic positioning
  - enable execution by mobilization of workforce *with* employees
- Use offshoring for *all* strategic dimensions (cost, new markets, learning, increased reach through partners)
- Seek win-wins with community
- Proactively communicate with and educate society
- Reach out to governments (from local to EU) and unions
- Don't ask for protection when convenient (it destroys credibility)

National Economic Competitiveness and Growth

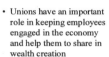

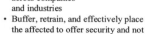

- Reduce product marke restrictions that reduce competition
- Reduce labor market restrictions to allow re-allocation of jobs across companies and industries
- Buffer, retrain, and effectively place the affected to offer security and not exclude them
- Experiment with local solutions for training and placement
- Decentralize education; allow local experiments and introduce competition
- Educate the public more openly about economic tradeoffs
- Make economic productivity a higher priority (because it drives growth)

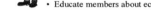

- Unions have an important role in keeping employees engaged in the economy and help them to share in wealth creation
- Recognize the importance of competitiveness and productivity
- Work as a partner of management
- Educate members about economic tradeoffs

Fig. 10.5. Summary of action directions

Of course, Europe still has a lot to offer – skills are still comparatively high, institutions, infrastructure, and company competitiveness are still world class. In the 2007 INSEAD-World Global Innovation Index, the US leads but five of the top ten countries are European (Germany, UK, France, Switzerland and the Netherlands).[37] Moreover, the latest labor productivity growth numbers indicate that Europe overtook the US (1.5% vs. 1.4%) in 2006, with Germany's improvement at 2% and the Scandinavian countries' at over 2.5%.[38] The evidence clearly shows that Europe, and particularly European firms, *can* compete on the world stage.

Thus, there is no reason to foresee doom, and there are signs that European economies are (slowly) responding. Indeed, in the late spring of 2007, the general mood in Europe seemed on its way to becoming much more optimistic.[39] However, it would be wrong to conclude from recent positive signs that all is well – much more needs to be done to respond to the competitiveness increase in Asia and not become a relative backwater. The European community cannot rest on its laurels at these faint signs of success. Nor are fatalism and hopelessness warranted. If everyone makes their mind up to it, Europe can prosper as much as ever.

---

[37] See Dutta and Caulkin 2007. The top ten countries are by rank: US, Germany, UK, Japan, France, Switzerland, Singapore, Canada, the Netherlands, Hong Kong.

[38] The Southern European countries (such as Italy, Spain and Portugal) showed weak productivity improvements below 1%. See the Conference Board 2007.

[39] de Weck 2007.

The message to management of European companies is: roll up your sleeves and achieve competitiveness with a combination of sustainable strategic positioning and management quality. That is your most important contribution to society. At the same time, do not neglect to communicate to the public what's going on – we remind the reader of the debate about excessive salaries and the clumsy execution of restructuring measures in Sect. 3. If the general population sees that they too can benefit from a shift in the mix of economic activities, change will become easier and more productive. Managers need to step up to the challenge of competitiveness, while being willing to be held accountable to high standards of ethical behaviour. Anything less will justify the voices protesting against "globalization" and "capitalism" and asking for more regulation.

Globalization is inevitable; the result of blocking it would lead to more poverty everywhere. But the focus of this book is not globalization and off-shoring. This book shows how management can achieve competitiveness through management quality and strategic positioning, and in collaboration with societal partners. If firms engage in this dialogue and collaboration they will bring along change far more effectively than by just complaining about unions and politicians.

References

Aiginger, K. 2002. Growth Difference Between Europe and the US in the 1990s: Causes and Likelihood of Persistence. European Forum Working Paper, Stanford University.

Algan, Y., Cahuc, P. 2006. Civic Attitudes and the Design of Labor Market Institutions: Which Countries Can Implement the Danish Flexicurity Model? Institute for the Study of Labor (IZA) Working Paper 1928.

Berg, A., Gottschalg, O. 2003. Understanding Value Generation in Buyouts. INSEAD Working Paper 2003/42/sm.

Bergoeing, R., Kehoe, T. J., Strauss-Kahn, V., Yi, K. -M. 2004. Why Is Manufacturing Trade Rising Even as Manufacturing Output Is Falling? Federal Reserve Bank of Philadelphia Research Working Paper 04-4.

Bonini, S. M. J., Mendonca, L. T., Oppenheim, J. M. 2006. When Social Issues Become Strategic. The McKinsey Quarterly 2/2006, 20–32.

Boston Consulting Group. 2004. Produktionsstandort Deutschland – Quo Vadis? White Paper.

Brander, J., Hendricks, K., Amit, R., Whistler, D. 1998. The Engine of Growth Hypothesis: On the Relationship Between Firm Size and Employment Growth. Working paper, The University of British Columbia, Vancouver.

Buch, C. M., Schnitzer, M. 2007. Analyse der Beweggründe, der Ursachen und der Auswirkungen des so genannten Offshoring auf Arbeitsplätze und Wirtschaftsstruktur in Deutschland. Report, Institut für angewandte Wirtschaftsforschung, Tübingen, Ludwig Maximiliansuniversität München.

Cao, J. X., Lerner, J. 2006. The performance of reverse leveraged buyouts. Boston College/ Harvard University and National Bureau of Economic Research Working Paper, October.

Charan, R., Tichy, N. M. 1998. *Every Business is a Growth Business*. Chichester: Wiley.

Collins, J. 2001. *Good to Great – Why Some Companies Make the Leap and Others Don't*. New York: Harper Collins.

The Conference Board. 2007. US Productivity Growth in Slowdown. www.conference-board.org.

De la Fuente, A., Domenech, R. 2000. Human Capital in Growth Regressions: How Much Difference Does Data Quality Make? OECD Economics Department Working Papers #262.

de Weck, R. 2007. Der deutsche Frühling. Der Spiegel, May 15, 79.

Doz, Y., Santos, J., Williamson, P. 2001. *From Global to Metanational: How Companies Win in the Knowledge Economy*. Boston: Harvard Business School Press.

Dutta, S., Caulkin, S. 2007. The World's Top Innovators. World Business, January–February, 26–37.

Dutta, S., Larsen, P. F. 2006. The Finnish Miracle. World Business, May, 56–59.

The Economist. 2005. The Darkest Hour before Dawn: Deutschland AG is Starting to Look like a Bargain. August 4.

The Economist. 2005b. Manufacturing Employment: Industrial Metamorphosis. October 1, 69–70.

The Economist. 2007. In the Shadow of Prosperity. January 20, 30–32.

The Economist. 2007b. The uneasy crown (briefing private equity). February 10, 73–75.

The Economist 2007c. Private Equity: Less Taxing. February 17, 74–75.

The Economist 2007d. Economics Focus: Smaller Share, Bigger Slices. April 7, 72.

Ehrensberger, W. 2006. Betriebsrat gegen 40-Stunden-Woche: Arbeitnehmervertreter von Fujitsu Siemens fordern Einsparung in der Verwaltung. Die Welt, July 18.

Farrell, D. 2004. How Germany Can Win from Offshoring. McKinsey Quarterly (4), 114–123.

Feenstra, R. C., Hanson, G. H. 1999. The Impact of Outsourcing and High-Technology Capital on Wages: Estimates for the United States. Quarterly Journal of Economics 114 (3), 907–940.

Häcki, R., Lighton, J. 2001. The Future of the Networked Company. McKinsey Quarterly (3), 26–39.

Handelsblatt 2007. Das Trugbild "Flexicurity." Handelsblatt December 17, 9.

Hofer, J. 2007. Fujitsu Siemens bleibt gelassen. Handelsblatt, November 8.

Institut für Demoskopie Allensbach. 2004. Abwanderung von UNyternehemen: Wahrnehmung und Problembewusstsein der Öffentlichkeit. Presentation to the Press October 21.

Jørgensen, M. 2005. Boosting Growth through Greater Competition in Denmark. OECD Economic Department Working Paper No. 431.

Köcher, R. 2007. Der selektive Aufschwung. Frankfurter Allgemeine Zeitung February 21, 2007, 5.

Kröher, M. 2007. Professor Sonnenschein. ManagerMagazin (1), 110–115.

Krugman, P. 1997. Raspberry for Free Trade. Slate (The Dismal Science Column), November 20.

Lambeth, J. 1999. Siemens and Fujitsu combine under PC margin pressure. Vnunet.com, June 16.

Lewis, W. W. 2004. The Power of Productivity. McKinsey Quarterly (2).

Loch, C. H. 2008. Mobilizing an R&D organization through strategy cascading. Research Technology Management, in press.

Loch, C. H., Chick, S., Huchzermeier, A. 2007. Can European Manufacturing Companies Compete? Industrial Competitiveness, Employment and Growth in Europe. European Management Journal 25(4), 251–265.

Loch, C. H., Kavadias, S. 2007. *Handbook of New Product Development Management*. London: Butterworth Heineman.

Loch, C. H., Van der Heyden, L., Van Wassenhove, L. N., Huchzermeier, A., Escalle, C. X. 2003. *Industrial Excellence*. Berlin Heidelberg New York: Springer.

Loch, C. H., Wu, Y. 2006. Zyme Solutions: High Value Outsourcing. INSEAD Case 07/2006-5388.

ManagerMagazin 1999. Geteiltes Leid. ManagerMagazin 8/99, 10.

Milne, R. 2006. German Blue Chips Fear Eastern Rivals. Financial Times, August 29, 23.

Milne, R., Williamson, H. 2006. Selective Bargaining: German Companies are Driving a Hidden Revolution in Labour Flexibility. Financial Times, January 6, 9.

Mokyr, J. 1990. *The Lever of Riches*. Oxford: Oxford University Press.

Müller, H. 2006. Die Lehrstellenlüge. ManagerMagazin 9/2006, 98–104.

Müller, H. 2006b. Über den Wolken. ManagerMagazin 3/2006, 105–111.

Müller, H., D. Student. 2006. Viele hassen Big Business: Interview mit McKinsey's Ian Davis. ManagerMagazin 7/2006, 102–110.

Nicoletti, G., Scarpetta, S. 2003. Regulation, Productivity and Growth: OECD Evidence. Economic Policy 18 (36), 9–72.

OECD (Editor). 2006. Local Economic and Employment Development Skills Upgrading: New Policy Perspectives. OECD, ISBN 9264012508.

OECD. 2006. Education at a Glance: OECD Indicators 2006. OECD Publishing.

Politi, J., Guerrera, F. 2007. Private road to nowhere? Buyout teams face a bumpy ride now raising debt is hard. Financial Times, December 21, 5.

Porter, M. E. 1990. *The Competitive Advantage of Nations*. New York: The Free Press.

Saint-Paul, G. 2004. The Brain Drain: Some Evidence from European Expatriates in the United States. GREMAQ-IDEI, Université de Toulouse 1, CEPR, and IZA Working Paper.

Sauga, M., Aden, M., Brenner, J., Matthes, S. Die wahre Unterschicht. Der Spiegel 14/2007, 22–38.

Stevenson, M. 2007. Clever stuff: education and skills are Britain's weak spots. The Economist, February 3, Special Report on Britain, 9–11.

Strauss-Kahn, V. 2003. The Role of Globalization in the Within-Industry Shift away from Unskilled Workers in France. NBER WP 9716.

Utterback, J. 1996. *Mastering the Dynamics of Innovation*. Boston: Harvard Business School Press.

Westergaard-Nielsen, N. 2001. Danish Labour Market Policy: Is it Worth it? Centre for Labour Market and Social Research Department of Economics, The Aarhus School of Business Working Paper 01-10.

Williamson, H. 2008. Germany steps up Nokia protests. *Financial Times*, January 19, 1.

About the Authors

Christoph Loch

INSEAD, Boulevard de Constance, 77305 Fontainebleau Cedex, France
christoph.loch@insead.edu

Christoph H. Loch is the Glaxo Smith Kline Chaired Professor of Corporate Innovation at INSEAD and the Dean of INSEAD's PhD program. His research revolves around the management of R&D, the product innovation process, technology strategy, project selection, concurrent engineering, project management under high uncertainty, performance measurement, and how to motivate professional employees (as in R&D).

Professor Loch has published widely in journals in technology and operations management and books on management quality in manufacturing, on managing highly novel projects, and a handbook of new product development. He handles executive seminars at INSEAD, is a consultant to European corporations on technology management, and serves on the supervisory board of an educational software start-up company. He holds a PhD in business from Stanford, an MBA from UT Knoxville, and a Diplom-Wirtschaftsingenieur degree from the Darmstadt Institute of Technology.

Stephen E. Chick

INSEAD, Boulevard de Constance, 77305 Fontainebleau Cedex, France
stephen.chick@insead.edu

Steve Chick is Professor of Technology and Operations Management at INSEAD. He received his BS from Stanford, worked for five years in the automotive and software industries, and then obtained his PhD from the University of California at Berkeley. After serving on the faculty at the University of Michigan, he joined INSEAD in 2001. Professor Chick teaches operations management and service operations in the MBA program, process and simulation modeling in the PhD program, and operations management in executive education programs, particularly for the healthcare sector.

Professor Chick's research and teaching focus on production and operations management, operational excellence, health care delivery and policy, and simulation analysis for manufacturing and health care systems. He serves or has served in editorial positions for *Operations Research*, *Management Science*, and other leading journals. He is currently President of the Institute for Operations Research and Management Science (INFORMS) Simulation Society.

Arnd Huchzermeier

WHU-Otto Beisheim School of Management, Burgplatz 2, 56179 Vallendar, Germany
arnd.huchzermeier@whu.edu

Arnd Huchzermeier holds the Chair in Production Management of the Otto-Beisheim School of Management of the WHU in Vallendar. He received his PhD degree from the Wharton School, and has frequently taught at the University of Chicago and the Wharton School. His research interests include production and service operations management with a strong focus on management quality, global supply chain management and the evaluation of real options. He has published in leading international academic journals, and serves as associate editor of Management Science and Production and Operations Management.

He is a member of the board of the International Commerce Institute of ECR Europe and Executive Editor of the International Commerce Review. He has won numerous awards, such as the 2003 ISMS Practice Prize from the Marketing Science Institute, the 2003 Management Science Strategic Innovation Prize from the European Associations of Operational Research Societies, the 2002 Franz Edelman Finalist Award from the Institute of Operations Research and Management Science, and the 2000 Mercurius Award from Fedis, the European Federation of Distribution Societies.

Index

Main sections in **bold**
Diagrams in *italics*